THE POLITICAL PARTY MATRIX

D1713156

SUNY series in Political Party Development
Edited by Susan J. Tolchin

The Political Party Matrix

The Persistence of Organization

J. P. Monroe

STATE UNIVERSITY OF NEW YORK PRESS

Published by
State University of New York Press, Albany

For information, address State University of New York Press,
90 State Street, Suite 700, Albany, NY 12207

Production by Cathleen Collins
Marketing by Michael Campochiaro

Library of Congress Cataloging in Publication Data

Monroe, J. P., 1962-
    The political party matrix : the persistence of organization / J. P. Monroe.
        p.   cm. — (SUNY series in political party development)
    Includes bibliographical references (p.   ) and index.
    ISBN 0-7914-4917-3 (alk. paper) — ISBN 0-7914-4918-1 (pbk. : alk.
paper)
        1. Political parties—United States.   I. Title.   II. Series.
JK2261.M57 2001
324.273'11-dc21   00-040019

10   9   8   7   6   5   4   3   2   1

Contents

Preface

This book began out of a sense of frustration with the debate over the health of American political parties. The parties are experiencing significant change, yet little of the research reflects a sensitivity to the adaptive properties of political parties. It seems that our traditional assumptions of what constitute the legitimate components of a political party have become a barrier to understanding the scope and nature of party change. Our presuppositions about how parties should be organized and what functions they should perform caused us to forget what we have always known about American political parties: American parties are fluid and elastic institutions.

Despite the constraints imposed by the need for parties to parallel the complex structures of government, and the variability of these constraints by location, they display a remarkable capacity to adapt to a variety of unique settings. The theme of this book is simple: despite the popular perception that American political parties are defective institutions, the parties' adaptive properties continue to make them effective agents in the political system.

This study focuses on political parties in California, specifically in the greater Los Angeles area. California is often described as particularly fallow ground for those attempting to organize the parties. It is where the initiative process first gained a foothold; it is where campaign consultants first plied their trade and gave birth to a new industry. Since the turn of the century, like nowhere else in the United States, California constrained, controlled, and restricted the parties' presence in the political arena. In spite of these barriers, the parties continue to thrive.

This study is based on several sources. The first is a project conducted at UCLA with my colleagues Dwaine Marvick, John R. Petrocik, and Fernando J. Guerra in the winter of 1990. The project conducted interviews with over 300 field staffers working for incumbents from Congress, the California State Senate and Assembly, the Los Angeles County Board Supervisors, and the Los Angeles City Council. In all, over 100 offices took part in the study.

The second source is additional interviews that I conducted in the winter of 1992. These interviews were designed to supplement the information gathered in the first study and provide greater detail on Los Angeles party politics. These interviews focused on three different groups. I first conducted interviews with the chiefs-of-staff in the field offices for members of Congress and the State Assembly in and around Los Angeles County. Together, I interviewed fifty chiefs-of-staff, twenty-two from congressional offices and twenty-eight from the California State Assembly. The second group that I interviewed was the political consultants who worked for the national and state elected officials in my interview sample. I interviewed a total of thirty consultants. The final set of interviews were with the Democratic and Republican Central Committee party chairs for Los Angeles, Orange, Ventura, San Bernardino, and Riverside counties. Each county has a Democratic and Republican chair, for a total of ten interviews.

A detailed description of the interview sample and method is provided in the appendix along with the questionnaires.

Acknowledgements

I would like to thank John Petrocik for his encouragement and guidance throughout this project. The School of Business at the University of Miami generously provided funding that gave me time to finish the book.

I also thank the many professionals working in the field offices for elected officials in Southern California. Without the gift of their time and insight, the book could not have been completed.

Finally, I owe a debt of gratitude to Terrie, my wife, for her love and support.

1

American Political Parties

State of Decay, Reorganization, or Holding Their Own?

Sentence first—verdict afterward.
—Lewis Carroll, *Alice's Adventures in Wonderland*

A merican political parties are alive and well, despite a widespread belief in and out of academia that they are dead, or not far from it. The parties are adaptable institutions, and far from declining in importance, the parties continue to be the principal link between citizens and elites in the struggle for control over the formal institutions of government.

Our fragmented and limited understanding of political parties has contributed to the inaccurate view that the parties are declining. Little research has addressed the problem of party transformation from the perspective of whether the disappearance of certain party structures might mean that the parties have opted for superior forms of organization. In short, there seems to a general lack of appreciation for the adaptive qualities of political parties.

Our understanding of political parties is clearly deficient. The study of political parties has always been at the core of our discipline. One reason for this enduring tradition in political science is that political parties offer the scholar an excellent way to study the politics of our nation. However, the extensive body of the literature on parties belies what we have still to learn about them. The collective work on political parties exists in isolated units, divided by an inability to agree on theoretically relevant concepts. Therefore, we cannot agree what is worth knowing about the parties. We simply lack the conceptual tools for sorting out all there is to learn about them.

Yet lacking a sound theoretical base for studying the parties is only part of the problem. Perhaps even more troubling is that there is little appreciation for disarray that characterizes the research on the parties. With few exceptions, scholars continue to study and talk about the parties as if terms like "party" and "party organization" had some universal meaning. Debate about

1

the nature of political parties would seem appropriate during a period of party transformation, yet much of the research on the parties is all but silent on these issues.

The terms "party," "organization," and "party organization" produce many, and often vague, expectations about party activities and structures. The assumptions that stand behind these expectations often predetermine the scope of party existence: how it is structured, those who are counted among its membership, and the functions that it is allowed to perform. Each of the above terms also conveys a rich and elaborate set of ideas, images, and values about what political parties *were*, what they *are*, and what they *ought to be*.

The absence of appropriate and applicable party concepts has further resulted in the inability to place the information that we do have in a coherent theory of the party. Therefore, we are unable to generalize about the party as an institution, which differentiates itself from other institutions like interest groups or labor unions. E. E. Schattschneider's criticism of the study of parties still rings true today:

> The study of political parties has been remarkably confused by the poverty of the English language as far as the vocabulary of politics is concerned. Organizations called 'parties' at various times in various places have in fact been fundamentally dissimilar, but all alike have been called parties for want of a sufficient variety of words corresponding to the diversity of realities. The label has therefore been attached to many different things. (1942, 65)

Our judgments about party change and transformation are unfortunately entangled with a superficial acceptance of the meaning of the terms "party" and "organization." Many of our contemporary pronouncements about the health of American parties proceed from a sketchy understanding of the nature of political parties.

In addition, we have used an inappropriate benchmark, the nineteenth-century party machine, as a starting point for too much of the research on the parties in the United States. An unmistakable nostalgia for parties from the Golden Age of Politics colors much of the criticism of contemporary parties. I would argue, however, that this is as much a story about our limited understanding of the nature of political parties as it is any real or perceived defects that contemporary parties are claimed to possess. I put forth a definition of political parties, with evidence to support it, that permits a more critical assessment of the current state of American political parties.

Before exploring these and other issues, a brief discussion of the current state of research on the parties follows.

PARTY DECLINE

From the time of Walter Dean Burnham's 1969 article, "The End of American Party Politics," we have been aware that the party system has been experiencing a transformation. The nature and scope of this change have dominated party research throughout the 1980s; however, whether this change means that we will have a moribund party system or a reinvigorated one has yet to be settled by political scientists. The debate on the health of the parties has swung like a pendulum from a position that documented the breakdown of the parties on several fronts to one that argued that pronouncements of the party's demise were premature.

Throughout the 1970s and the early part of the 1980s, scholars were calling on party observers to witness the decline or death of the American political parties (Burnham 1982, 1970; Dennis 1980; see especially Pomper 1977). Many scholars argued that both parties—Democratic and Republican— no longer fulfilled the necessary role of linking citizens with government. PACs, single-issue groups, and political consultants competed with American parties in mobilizing constituents, defining policy, running campaigns, and raising and spending money (Crotty 1984). Additionally, the growing independence of the parties' candidates in campaigns presumably provided apt testimony to the decline of the party as an organizing force in elections (Polsby 1983; Kirkpatrick 1977; Crotty and Jacobson 1980). Moreover, the decline of party as a symbol in the minds of voters suggested that parties were no longer perceived as vehicles for transforming popular grievances into public policy; fewer and fewer voters identified with the parties and the degree of intensity of existing identifications declined (Wattenberg 1998; Ladd 1978; Nie et al. 1976).

The concern for the decline of party did not develop out of thin air. The evidence from studies on the party-in-the-electorate concluded that the parties were experiencing significant change. Party identifiers had dramatically decreased and split-ticket voting had become common (Crotty and Jacobson 1984). Scholars also mustered evidence detailing the unraveling of the New Deal party system (e.g., Petrocik 1981). Other changes in the political system also raised concerns that the parties-as-institutions were declining. Both parties experienced a series of reforms in the early part of the 1970s that, many argued, reduced their role in the electoral process (e.g., Polsby 1983).

THE PARTY RESURGENCE: THE EVIDENCE

However, by the middle of the 1980s, many scholars were identifying either signs of party resurgence (Reichley 1985; Herrnson 1986; Kayden and Mahe

1985) or arguing that the parties never really declined (Cotter et al. 1984; Schlesinger 1985). Several scholars point to the strengthening of the parties' national committee structure (Frantzich 1989; Luntz 1988; Kayden and Mahe 1987; Herrnson 1986; Reichley 1985; Price 1984; Longley 1980). According to these authors, both parties have developed an extensive campaign-oriented service apparatus that provides fund raising, candidate training, and campaign strategy. The Republican party placed the most resources in this service structure with a great deal of electoral success (Price 1984). Michael Malbin reported that "a new Republican organization has emerged—a multimillion dollar bureaucracy that employs 350 and plays an increasingly important role in all aspects of Republican campaigning and party policy" (1980; as quoted in Price 1984, 40). Stephen Frantzich (1989) emphasizes the Republican party development of a "service-vendor" apparatus that provides money and expertise to national and state candidates alike. Many now argue that the parties have strong national institutions, perhaps the strongest in United States history.

The emergence of this service apparatus began during the 1970s when Republicans redoubled their efforts to use the national committee to strengthen ties with the state committees. As a result, the Republican National Committee enforced changes in the structure of the state committees; it coordinated resources such as direct mail; and it even had some success in integrating the campaign messages used by its congressional candidates (Herrnson 1986). Trying to keep up with their rivals, the Democratic National Committee also developed a service apparatus, but in the past they have concentrated their efforts on enforcing the procedures and rules governing delegate selection to the national convention. However, Republican successes have spurred the Democrats to create a campaign-oriented apparatus of their own. In addition, although it has been a particularly Democratic enthusiasm, both parties have established liaison offices that deal with specific minority groups.

Along with these developments at the national level, the current condition of state and local party institutions does not support simplistic generalizations about party decline (Frendreis and Gitelson 1998; Frendreis 1996; Frendreis, Gibson, and Vertz 1990). Cornelius Cotter and his colleagues studied the transformation of state parties and have found that, paradoxically, the decline in party identification, the rise of a new breed of party professionals, and the "institutionalization" of the state parties seem to have occurred simultaneously (Gibson et al. 1985; Cotter et al. 1984; Gibson et al. 1983). They discover that, during this period of reputed party decay, state and local parties have increased their activities, and rather than experiencing decline, the parties have been undergoing steady growth over the last several decades.

CHARACTERIZING THE "RESURGENT" PARTY

Challenges to the party decline thesis have met some resistance (e.g., Coleman 1994, 1996). Much of the criticism arises out of the belief that the resurgent literature overstates the organizational strength of the parties and party scholars have failed to adequately address the continuing decline of the party-in-the-electorate. In other words, decreasing levels of partisanship in the electorate belie any resurgent trends. However, the conceptual difficulty of trying to consider trends in mass political behavior as an attribute of parties arises in such studies as Wattenberg's *The Decline of American Political Parties* (1998). The decision to equate declining voter loyalty as synonymous with declining parties rather than declining partisanship clearly implies a belief that the parties are responsible for the trend. I would argue that there is a conceptual problem with this approach.

Most would assume that the condition of parties as organizations and the party-in-the electorate are independent, but interlocking phenomenon, that is, the state of one has an influence on the other. However, few would argue that is it is perfect relationship. It is not difficult to envision a series of exogenous factors that would push levels of party loyalty down without changes in party activity. For example, rising levels of education and the emergence of a middle class in the American electorate has been linked to lower levels of partisanship. Neither of these could be regarded as failures on the part of the parties to respond to political or institutional change.

This is not to suggest that there is no relationship between the activities of the parties and the attitudes of voters. However, the proposition that the behavior of parties and the attitudes of voters are related should not imply that other factors may be responsible for a decline in partisanship—factors that do not indicate party failure or insignificance. In fact, the opposite may be true: the well-documented decline of partisanship in the 1960s and 1970s may have been offset or slowed by a "resurgent" party. In other words, a more vigorous level of activity on the part of the party may have slowed or even reversed an exogenously determined decline in partisanship. What remains is a paradox or a puzzle that requires further research. While the connection to voter attitudes is important, most party scholars have focused on what these changes mean for the parties as organizations.

What is the meaning of these developments in party change? The contradictory data—the disintegration of the parties' support among voters, the increasingly bureaucratized national and state parties, and the increasing professionalization of the consulting business—have engendered a variety of conflicting interpretations about the place of parties in the political process. Some continue to insist that the parties are still experiencing a decline (Coleman 1994, 1996; Crotty 1985). Others have begun to study candidate-centered campaigns as the central variable in party research (Gimpel 1996; Goldberg and Traugott 1984; Hershey 1984; Jacobson 1983). Some now argue that we have a "new" party system based on the ambitions of office seekers (Schlesinger 1985).

The contradictory evidence has initiated attempts to redefine the parties. Xandra Kayden and Eddie Mahe describe the party system as a "phoenix . . . risen from the ashes" (1985, 3). They argue that the use of national party resources to recruit and train candidates is more likely to create a cohesive party elite (1985, 196). Paul Herrnson (1986) introduced a new model for understanding the party based on his interviews with members of the Republican and Democratic Committees. He argues that the party has moved from the nineteenth-century "party-as-machine" model to a contemporary image of the "party-as-peripheral." He goes on to argue, however, that the provision of campaign resources from the committees of the national parties has created a new (and weaker) role for the "party-as-broker." This is similar to Stephen Frantzich's (1989) argument that the parties have quickly developed a "service-vendor" role in their support of candidates for federal offices. In a similar vein, Christopher Arterton proposed a "PAC" model of the parties (1982, 132). He identifies the increasing role that the parties now play in the channeling of funds to candidates as a key development, minimizing the effects of the candidate-centered campaign. He warns, however, that a strengthened national party probably can effectively use the new technologies, but the national committees are unable to replace the parties at the local level as channels for citizen demands (1982, 136).

Perhaps the most widely known effort to redefine the party has been put forth by Cornelius Cotter, James Gibson, John Bibby, and Robert Huckshorn (1984) in which the party is thought to have experienced an institutional rebirth, an increase in the bureaucratization of the formal institutions of the party at the state and national levels. This "new institutionalization" of the party is based on the idea that the parties have strengthened their formal institutions by becoming more bureaucratized as a way of offsetting the decomposition or decline in one sector of the party, the party-in-the-electorate. In effect, the parties have combated changes in the electorate through the development of a party bureaucracy.

EVALUATING THE "NEW ORTHODOXY"

The weight of evidence from recent party research suggests that the parties are now more national in scope; there is greater integration between the electoral efforts of the national and state parties; and both parties have resisted trends leading to decline by becoming more "institutionalized." This has produced a new benchmark that many party observers use to evaluate party strength and effectiveness: the bureaucratic party. As a result, the parties are increasingly scrutinized for signs of bureaucratic development, and thus, concepts of *bureaucratic organization* are steadily supplanting concepts of *party organization*. However, these efforts to redefine the parties as bureaucratic institutions are inadequate. The party's formal apparatus may share some similarities with a bureaucracy, as many scholars insist, but a nagging question of pertinence confronts us: given the circumscribed nature of this standard, is prodding the parties for signs of bureaucratic life the way we should be studying the parties?

The shift to studying parties as cousins of bureaucratic institutions has several problems. First, while the increase in bureaucratization of the party appears systematic, the emphasis on formal developments in the party's structure does little to answer the question about the institutional basis of the party. This approach divorces notions of party effectiveness from their role in the electoral process. In short, we are not told what a party bureaucracy is good for. They present no standards needed to evaluate the consequences of the development of a party bureaucracy. The only appropriate test for the strength and effectiveness of these "new" party structures is how well they help the parties win elections. Concepts like party "effectiveness" and "strength" have no meaning beyond an electoral test. What are consequences of the party's bureaucracy for electoral activity or the party's success at the polls? What success do they have at the recruitment of viable candidates for office? How well does the overarching structure of the formal apparatus coordinate the parties' efforts at different levels of government?

Second, we should pause to consider if a party bureaucracy is typical of most American political parties, and whether the weight we attach to this change is justified. American parties of the past were organizationally spare, having few (if any) of the features that many scholars now deem important indicators of party strength. A bureaucracy may be an unrealistic and inappropriate standard by which to analyze the party's structure. In the past, linkages in the party's structure were informal in nature. An informal system of reciprocity and autonomy linked party leaders to each another, and this seldom (if ever) conformed to a bureaucratic style of organization. Even the urban political machines of the past, with their multiple layers of organization, were not bureaucratically structured. The urban machines sometimes had access to sanctions with which it could enforce discipline, and the structure of the machines was occasionally hierarchical, but these parties were not bureaucracies. And there is little indication that it applies to the parties today.

The preoccupation with the emergence of a party bureaucracy may cause us to emphasize aspects of party development that are less relevant than others. Parties at the state level exhibit only a few of the telltale signs of bureaucratic development, and parties at the local level hardly at all (Jewel and Olson 1988). Gibson et al. (1985, 155) report that most local parties are *not* bureaucratically organized and the strength of local party institutions is independent of the strength of the state party institutions as measured by their bureaucratic complexity (See also Cotter et al. 1984, 16). Local parties remain non-bureaucratic in structure and do not conform to the model that many party resurgent scholars are using as a standard for evaluating the weakness or strength of the party.

Third, this redefinition of the party invariably focuses on the increased professionalization among the staff of the parties' formal apparatus, almost to the exclusion of the informal aspects of the parties' structure. Certainly, the professionalization of the party makes it more sophisticated, reflecting the needs of the modern campaign; however, screened from view are the multitude of efforts to win office in the party's name below the level of the national and state apparatus. This grows out of a circumscribed definition of what constitutes the institutional basis of the party.

A bureaucratic conceptualization of the party recognizes those in formal party positions—party chairs, their professional staffs, and other workers "officially" linked with the apparatus. However, the party effort in the recruitment of candidates, in elections, and in the coordination of governmental activity is not confined (or even centered) in these formal party structures. In the end, a bureaucratic approach to the party may tell us little about how the party accomplishes a variety of critical tasks. Much of the party's activity occurs within an institution characterized by informal relationships between the party elite, yet this represents an important aspect of the party's structure. It is unlikely that a bureaucratic model captures these activities that are important to the survival of the party. Without an ability to describe and explain this process, our understanding of the institutional basis of the party can only be a partial one.

Political parties are unlike any other large bureaucratic institutions (Eldersveld 1964). A bureaucracy is a unique style of organization, requiring clear lines of jurisdiction, formalization of relationships between those in the institution, specialization of institutional tasks through the division of labor, and a centralized authority structure. Political parties should, therefore, not be confused with an institutional copy of a bureaucracy. As Samuel Eldersveld argued many years ago:

> Although party leadership cadres may indeed have some esprit de corps, this is quite different from that of a bureaucratic cadre. In the latter case, esprit de corps rests heavily on vocational security, professional associations, expectations of permanency, and a desire to protect the group from its environment. The party, however, is

an open structure; tenure is unstable; personal relationships are uncertain. Thus power vanishes easily within a political party. . . . (1964, 11)

To equate the party with a bureaucracy is to constrain the party to a structure that may bear little resemblance to reality. To view this as the only relevant shift in party development is to obscure other significant changes that are also occurring. Rather than using a bureaucratic model as a guide to the party's structure, we should perhaps reevaluate our understanding of the nature of parties and party institutions.

Schlesinger's observation, made over thirty years ago, is still relevant today: "Although political parties provide the basis for the study of organizations for such pioneers as Michels (1949), Ostrogorski (1902), and Weber (1958) parties stand outside the mainstream of organizational theory" (Schlesinger 1965, 764). A complete understanding of the party's institution must include not only an awareness of the changes that have occurred in the party's formal apparatus, but we must also have an understanding of the informal structure of the party. Yet a preoccupation with the legally defined party apparatus dominates research on political party organizations. This does not mean that the formal apparatus is unimportant, rather a complete understanding of the party's institution must include an account of the informal aspects of its structure. To do otherwise is to misjudge the present state of American political parties.

THE MODERN POLITICAL PARTY

This book investigates the relationship between political staffing as a publicly funded institution and the modern political party. I will argue that cooperative linkages maintained between office holders are a crucial component of the modern party's structure. In the past, research on political parties emphasized the importance of the informal nature of the party's institutional arrangements. E. E. Schattschneider argued that "the extralegal character of political parties is one of their most notable qualities" (1942, 11).

The modern party has three components. The first is the campaign-oriented service apparatus at the national and state levels of the party. This component of the party includes the party chairs, the executive committee, party workers, and those specialists providing campaign expertise to the candidates through the formal apparatus of the party. It is this component of the party that has received the most attention among those arguing that the parties are experiencing an institutional resurgence. However, the following two components are just as vital to understanding what has been happening to the parties.

The second component of the modern party is the cadre of political consultants and campaign specialists. They are the technical and professional corps of the modern party, enhancing the party's ability to wage effective campaigns. Beyond working in the campaign, this cadre of professionals plays a significant role in the recruitment of candidates for public office, in the coordination of efforts between candidates during the campaign, and they even participate in the governing structure of the party (Sabato 1981; Luntz 1988; Salmore and Salmore 1985). My definition of a political party (presented in the next chapter) includes these participants tied to the party in less "official" ways. An evaluation of the party's structure would be incomplete without including those who make significant contributions to the party effort in elections. Moreover, to include only formally-specified party activists in a definition of the party is to ignore the extralegal nature of American political parties. These unofficial members are only isolated participants until they are seen as occupying integral positions in the party through the provision of vital technical and professional expertise. It is useful to think of a political party as having a technical core providing campaign services to candidates for public office.

The third component of the modern party (and the primary focus of this book) is the personal political apparatus of elected officials in national, state, and local public offices. Incumbents now command an unprecedented array of resources with which to set up district offices and hire staffs to provide constituent services and to help with their legislative duties. Political staffing is key to the incumbent's ability to build and maintain a personal political apparatus. Elected officials have truly become *enterprises-in-office*.[1]

The emergence of a sizable cadre of political staff has changed the structure of the modern party. The presence of the incumbent's political apparatus at the local, state, and national levels of government makes possible the elaborate coordination of electoral activity, since the linkages between these individual office holder units are an important structural component of the party. Therefore, the desire, willingness, or the need to coordinate activity creates a network of incumbent-based political units working to achieve influence over electoral outcomes. Because these office holder apparatuses exist at every level of government, the party-as-an-institution extends into different spheres of responsibility.

At the center of this system is the incumbent's personal political apparatus. Office holders now have the resources to consolidate power within the party, and not surprisingly, they have been best placed to coordinate the electoral efforts of the party across the various levels of government. The notion of "party" carries with it the idea of an institutional system that reaches into a multitude of localities, has a presence in more that one political and governmental arena, and entails cooperation with more than one institutional component. The emergence of the personal political apparatus with the capability of shifting resources to other efforts to capture political office reflects a party's essential institutional character: the party is a complex institution for the coordination of political efforts across extended governmental domains.

For example, members of Congress collaborate to influence state-level elections; state legislators combine their efforts with members of Congress to help candidates at the local level; and local officials will lend a hand in national races. They may contribute campaign funds, lend out their staff, or provide other forms of campaign expertise to aid in the efforts of others in the party. The collaborative efforts between office holders have always been an important feature of American political parties. But these linkages between office holders require renewed scholarly emphasis because, I argue, the collaboration between office holders has become essential to the understanding of how the parties are adapting to a world without old-style patronage and to a technologically-driven electoral system.

THE INSTITUTIONALIZATION OF THE WARD HEELER: POLITICAL STAFF

This study examines the adaptive characteristics of the parties' institutional base. In particular, I will present evidence of the campaign tasks performed by the incumbent's paid field staff.[2] The staffers under examination are those working in the field offices for members of Congress, state legislators, and local elected officials for the county and city government in the Los Angeles metropolitan area.

Since the emergence of the direct primary, office holders and office seekers have had to organize a personal network of supporters. State and national legislative candidates now assemble their own campaign team that handles fund raising, direct mail, polling, and hires consultants to design a campaign strategy. If a candidate is successful, members of this team often follow him into office. This is possible because incumbents now possess the resources to hire their own staff and to set up an elaborate district apparatus. Over the last several decades, elected officials at the national, state, and local levels of government have developed extensive district-based operations that engage in a variety of political activity.

Today, the publicly-funded personal political apparatus can be found at almost every level of government, assisting elected officials in their legislative roles. But this apparatus also has implications for the parties. This highly professional cadre of activists in the incumbents' district and legislative offices replaced the old-style patronage workforce. The modern political party, like those from a century ago, has developed a system that sustains a stable core of participants who can be counted on to engage in activities supportive of the parties' candidates for public office.

All previous studies of political staffing have concentrated on an institutional entity: the Senate, House, or the state legislature. This study, in contrast, will look at legislative staffs—federal, state, and local—within a single geographic, rather than institutional, entity. The emphasis here will be on field staffs and what they do back in the district, and the implications this has for the parties.

OVERVIEW OF THE BOOK

Though this is a study of the parties' structure in Los Angeles County, my goal in the book is to say something about the changing nature of parties in the United States. A variety of works illustrate the integral role that Washington staffs play in congressional operations (Fiorina 1977; Kofmehl 1977; Fox and Hammond 1977; Malbin 1979). Many scholars have noted the growing importance of the district-based field operation (e.g., Fiorina 1977; Fenno 1978; Macartney 1975; Cain et al. 1987). This includes the constituent service function of these district offices and their involvement in state and local electoral politics, but there has been little effort to reconcile this activity with some notion of the party. California is an ideal testing ground for the growth and development of new party structures. Traditional treatments of California politics generally conclude that California lacks strong parties, or at least the traditional forms of party organization prevalent in other parts of the United States. Therefore, my objective is to establish a benchmark, while extrapolating beyond California to say something about where American parties may be heading.

The unit of analysis for the study is the field offices of the elected officials in Los Angeles County, that is, members of Congress, California State Senators and members of the Assembly, Los Angeles County Board of Supervisors, and the Los Angeles City Council. With the high concentration of local, state, and national office holders in the county, including the generous level of staffing at each of these levels, Los Angeles County gives elected officials the potential to create and maintain considerable crosscutting institutions. With many other states establishing large, professional, and partisan staffs, Los Angeles County offers a glimpse of changes that may occur down the road for other areas of the country. It is important to keep in mind that this study is attempting to come to grips with a new kind of institution; this is not merely a study about Los Angeles politics.

The book is divided into two parts. The first (Chapters 1 through 3) includes a discussion of how the political science discipline has dealt with the topic of party, and in particular, the concept of party organization. The focus on the properties and components of a political party is crucial because, to understand what has been happening to the parties, we must have a clear conception of what a political party is: what criteria do we use to define its structure; what are the party's boundaries? Chapter 2 argues that some definitions have led many to conclude that the parties are experiencing an inexorable decline as a force in the political process. However, the definition put forth in this book suggests that these generalizations about the parties may be premature. Chapter 3 introduces my model of the new American party organization. This view of the party's institution is set in contrast to the traditional model used to judge contemporary parties, the nineteenth-century American political party. I will argue that insisting that modern parties adhere to a romanticized and glorified image of the party has hindered the development of theories of party change and transformation.

The second part (Chapters 4 through 7) examines the incumbent's enterprise-in-office. Each chapter examines a distinct function of the apparatus as a working component of the party. Chapter 4 examines some staff characteristics with a focus on their political ambitions, showing how staffing as an institution is altering recruitment patterns for those who seek public office. Chapter 5 details the level of staff involvement in electoral politics. Chapter 6 shows the significant efforts of incumbents to influence electoral outcomes through the lending of their staff and through the coordination of election plans with other candidates. It is this cooperative behavior that is the linchpin of the new party. Chapter 7 shows how the incumbent's district apparatus has evolved into a complex institution for solving constituency problems.

2

The Meaning of Party

You see, my position is slightly complicated because I'm not
just an elected official with the city; I'm a tribal chieftain as
well. It's a necessary dual kind of office holding, you might
say; without the second I wouldn't be the first.
—Edwin O'Connor, *The Last Hurrah*

THE SEARCH FOR PARTY

Political parties are mysterious creatures; the process of defining them draws
one into a tangle of preconceptions and normative concerns, and definitions are as numerous as the authors who write about the parties. They range
from simple statements incorporating some basic concepts, to more complex
efforts to cover all aspects of the party phenomenon by incorporating in a
single definition most of the functions parties perform.

Yet attempts to find a clear (and usable) definition of political parties
have thus far eluded political scientists. It has proven difficult to provide a
meaning of party that isolates its distinctive qualities, but retains its generaliz-
ability. The fluid interaction of parties with their environments, their frequently
diffuse structures, and the variety of settings in which they can be found frus-
trate easy definition of what a political party is.

Political parties have been defined in many ways, ranging from oligarchic associations (Michels 1949) to informal collections of candidates and
their followers, united to capture a single public office (Schlesinger 1984).
The choice of definition is important because different definitions have made
it possible for party observers to find signs of party deterioration on the one
hand (Pomper 1977; Wattenberg 1998; Burnham 1982; Crotty 1984) and
institutional resurgence on the other (Cotter et al. 1984; Kayden and Mahe
1987; Schlesinger 1985).

Some scholars insist that efforts to define parties are futile, arguing that
what is gained in theoretical power is certainly forfeited by excluding aspects
of party experience that lie outside certain "definitions" of the party. While

15

this criticism may have merit, the reverse runs the risk of continuing to study political parties without a sound theoretical base. The collective wisdom on the parties, then, becomes a body of interesting facts, trends, and data without any tools for sorting them out. We have no way of determining what is theoretically important and what, conversely, is extraneous information. We simply lack the instruments, leading to the differing conclusions about the health of the parties in America.

Through this process, party observers—journalists, party activists, and political scientists—have come to differing conclusions about what the parties are, what they ought to be, and the characteristics that differentiate them from other institutions. These competing judgments about the health of the parties are an unmistakable sign that what we know about the parties is deficient. This is the result of never having resolved the question: what is a political party? Before we pronounce contemporary parties as defective, it is critical that we proceed from a firm understanding of the nature of political parties.

Ideally, a definition should do more than describe everything we know about political parties. Many scholarly works on the parties present "definitions" that simply serve to organize their materials on the party, and others provide definitions that are only descriptions of party structures or activities. A more fruitful attack would begin by specifying a minimally acceptable definition. The strategy here is not to come up with a definition that encompasses the totality of party forms and activities, but to put forth a set of criteria that isolate uniform behavioral and structural characteristics that are essential to party existence.

The definition should answer the question: what are the requisite components that are essential to party existence? This should include characteristics that distinguish them from other institutions, and it should be testable. However, we must proceed with caution and heed V. O. Key's warning that "Pat definitions may simplify discussion but they do not necessarily promote understanding. A search for the fundamental nature of party is complicated by the fact that 'party' is a word of many meanings" (1964, 200).

Let me begin by presenting my working definition of party and party organization, and then turn to the different ways other scholars have studied the parties.

PARTY DEFINITION

Approaches to the study of political parties fall into two broad categories. The first conceptualizes party as an organized expression of citizens to alter the balance of power in the formal institutions of government. Elections are the primary arenas where citizens can express their support and dissatisfaction with the parties, registered in the competitive balance between them. This is a conception of party as an aggregation of the individuals and groups who support it. In a second approach, the party is an institution through which elites coordinate their activity as they attempt to satisfy the interests of their supporters. Thus, the party is a vehicle for the collaboration of activity as elites seek to control the formal institutions of government. While not disputing that parties can be viewed from its constituent parts using the first approach, this book squarely addresses questions relating to the institutional basis of the party, that is, the party's structural properties.

A political party is an institution through which elites coordinate their activities in elections and government as they attempt to satisfy the interests of their support base. Thus, this definition of party broadly prescribes the party's membership, and emphasizes the principles of office holding and office seeking as central variables in party theory. In particular, I draw from the theories of Anthony Downs (1957) and Joseph Schlesinger (1966; 1985). Both define parties in terms of office holders, office seekers, and their followers and assume that political elites act out of self-interest: "whether for power, prestige and income . . . or the love of conflict, i.e., the 'thrill of the game'" (Downs 1957, 30).

Party organization is the institutional consequence of the deliberate coordination of *activity* to win public office in the party's name. *Party organization is an institution organized to capture public office.* I argue that the institutional components of the party should be sought in terms of this activity, rather than in formal or bureaucratic structures.

This definition of party organization has three important elements. The first is that competing for electoral office is the preeminent goal of the party. Parties may seek other objectives, and participants in party affairs may derive a variety of benefits through their involvement; however, the definition offered here underscores the primacy of winning public office as the rationale for party existence. The second is that membership in the party's organization is defined in terms of electoral activity. I make no distinction between formally and informally specified participants, linkages, or activities. The third is that the institutional basis of the party (or its structure) is defined by the cooperative links between the party elite as they attempt to coordinate their activities in the electoral phase. Party organization is an institution structured by the task to be accomplished, and the major objective of the party is winning elections. As argued by E. E. Schattschneider,

> Parties are defined in terms of the bid for power because it is impossible to define them in terms of any other objective. (1942, 36)

It is not the commitment to a particular structure that characterizes the party's institution, but the activities that flow from it. This emphasizes the importance of specifying party organization in terms of electoral activity, rather than using formally prescribed structures.

The advantage of this approach is that the party is not bound to a particular structure or form, and it remains flexible enough to allow changes in the party's structure over time (Schlesinger 1985). Moreover, it narrows our focus to those players who contribute to the party's efforts to win elections; namely, candidates and their followers, including those people in and out of government who contribute time, money, and other resources to the party's effort to win elections. The party includes the candidates who hold and seek public office. It includes those people in government who work as members of the office holder's personal staff. It includes those out of government who work on campaigns such as pollsters, fund raisers, and media specialists. It includes those who hold formal party positions such as county chairs. Excluded from the party are those whom Schlesinger terms "essentially choosers among competing parties, i.e., the voters" (1984, 375).[1]

CENTRAL TASKS AND PARTY STRUCTURE

In attempting to delineate the properties of the modern party's institution, I assume that parties must perform certain vital tasks. At a minimum, these activities are: 1) the recruitment of candidates for public office, 2) the mobilization of voters in support of its candidates, and 3) the concentration of power within the formal institutions of the government.

To win elections or maintain power, parties find it necessary to appeal to their supporters. In addition, if they are to succeed at management in government, they must establish some connection between decision-makers in various agencies of government. These are the standards by which we can judge party effectiveness. This should not imply that parties do not perform other activities in the political system. Rather, I argue that these are critical to the party's effort to win elections. If the parties do other things in the political system, they do so as a consequence of these activities.

These activities draw us back to the party's preeminent goal of capturing public office. To be successful at the polls, parties must find viable candidates to run, they must find methods for ensuring that are supported by the voters, and they must use government to satisfy the desires of their supporters.

Parties are unique institutions because they are groups oriented to achieve specific goals under particular environmental conditions. The claim here is that parties do not possess a set of predetermined structural attributes. Rather, they must perform certain activities to survive, to be effective agents in the political system. Whether the party's structural properties support these activities may be open to question; however, this does not mean that parties must possess a particular structural or institutional form. Too often, research on the parties begins with an institutional benchmark stipulated by the researcher. Instead, I argue that we should use the activities performed by the party as a guide to its structure.

Therefore, a party should not be determined weak or strong based on whether it adheres to a predetermined structure. Rather, judgments about the parties should be based on whether it engages in certain activities, *whatever its structure.* Only then is it possible to face the question of how the party's components relate to one another, and by their *activities* create the party's structural properties.

STUDYING POLITICAL PARTIES

This study examines the structural basis of the party from a perspective that recognizes the adaptive characteristics of the parties. Doing so, however, requires a justification and the need to place the previous definition presented in the broader set of inquiries on political parties. This requires a review of the different ways that we as a discipline have attempted to define "party," the various meanings we have for "organization," and finally our numerous conceptions of "party organization."

Finding a satisfactory definition of party presents a significant challenge. It has been said that "it is perhaps easier to say what a party is not than to say what it is" (Commager 1950, 309). Clearly, there is a consensus that a party is more durable than a faction, is more extensive that a legislative voting bloc, and has different goals that an interest group. Beyond this point, however, various approaches have been employed by both political scientists and historians seeking a reasonable definition.

Some have provided only very loose definitions; examples include Binkley's (1958) characterization of parties as broad combinations of interest groups and Beard's (1915) use of the term to describe any group of people who generally share the same set of beliefs. But such weak definitions lead to ambiguous conclusions about the health of political parties: "They encourage evasion of distinctions between party and non-party politics, and leave unexposed questions which are basic to a theory of modern party politics" (Chambers 1963, 93). Fortunately, there are other definitions that more clearly differentiate parties from factions, voting blocs, or interest groups. Parties have been characterized by the activities or roles they perform in the political system (office-seeking or competing teams conception) or by the type of structures or organizational attributes they possess (organization conception).

THE COMPETING TEAMS OR OFFICE SEEKING CONCEPTION

This definition of the party begins with the premise that parties are distinguishable from other groups in the system by their capacity to contest and win elections. This perspective is not concerned with the issues that the parties represent, nor the nature of its constituent base, but is oriented toward finding political parties in terms of what they do—the activities associated with contesting elections. This is a peculiarly American definition of political parties, owing much to the loose, decentralized structure of most American party institutions.

Using this as a guide, American scholars have generally stressed the electoral characteristics of parties, emphasizing their efforts to capture public office through the recruitment and promotion of candidates who appeal to large segments of the voters. Edward Sait (1927), Austin Ranney (1975), and E. E. Schattschneider (1942) are good examples of this approach.

While holding steadfastly to the goal of democracy between strong parties, the "competing teams" advocates reject the need, or even the desirability, of democracy within the party and the commitment to a well-defined set of policy principles. It is ironic that the APSA report's chairman, E. E. Schattschneider, once argued that "Democracy is not to be found in parties but *between* the parties" (1942, 60). The competing teams approach is similar to Joseph Schumpeter's definition of a political party as a group "whose members propose to act in concert in the competitive struggle for political power" (1947, 283).

In an attempt to move this definition beyond the American political experience, Leon Epstein offers one that he claims will fit almost everything that is called a party in any Western democracy. He describes a party as "any group, however loosely organized, seeking to elect governmental office holders under a given label" (1983, 9). He believes having a "label" rather than an "organization" is the defining element, since this permits a group of aspiring office holders to seek voters under a collective label. One problem with this approach is that it merely describes the status quo without providing an explanation for it.

Some authors, like Anthony Downs, have been even more explicit in their attempt to confine parties to those who contribute to a candidate's effort to win public office. Most scholars have considered that voters are important participants in party affairs. However, Downs disagrees, insisting that parties consist of "teams" of "office holders." Therefore, he defines parties as "a team seeking to control the governing apparatus by gaining office in a duly constituted election" (1957, 25). According to Downs's definition, the party comprises elites who are seeking offices, and voters can be considered consumers who respond to public policy initiatives offered by competing sets of office seekers.

However, many scholars argue that voters are not rational all the time, and that the party is not always motivated by winning elections (e.g., Crotty 1984; Sorauf 1984; Pomper 1977). Downs offers a thought-provoking argument, but many political scientists are unable to accept its assumptions.

Critics of the "competing teams" approach argue that it is both too narrow and broad in its conception of political parties (e.g., Crotty 1986; Cotter et al. 1984). It is too narrow, they argue, because parties do more than contest elections. By defining parties as simply creatures of the electoral process, we lose many of the functions and activities that parties perform in political system. The definition is also thought to be narrowly conceived because it is a definition of American political parties, lacking relevance in other political settings. It is criticized as too broad because most of the "competing teams" definitions are so vague that almost anything can be a political party. It does not isolate those characteristics that distinguish parties from other groups that operate in the political arena, and it casts its theoretical net so wide that it is difficult to test its assumptions.

Each of these criticisms has merit; however, it is important to keep in mind that the approach does draw our attention to the central feature of the party: they are the only groups that contest elections. It is also useful to consider that, whatever else parties do, they do as a consequence of the electoral requirement.

Therefore, it is the task of those who wish to cast the party in terms of electorally-driven institutions to show what consequences arise from this requirement. In this way, a broad definition that considers parties as simply groups organized to win elections can be narrowed to include a predictable set of activities that flow from this fact.

THE ORGANIZATIONAL CONCEPTION

William Crotty observed that "Party organizational analysis is . . . one of the oldest in parties' research and one of the most frustrating" (1970, 281). One frustrating aspect of this approach is its idiosyncratic nature. The literature on the structure of political parties is rich and varied, ranging from the pioneering works of Michels (1949) and Ostrogorski (1921), through the European studies of Duverger (1954), Neumann (1956), and Kirchheimer (1966), and then the predominantly American work of Eldersveld (1964), Crotty (1986), Wright (1971) and Cotter et al. (1984). Yet each work introduces a new conceptual framework, resulting in what one author has criticized as "a confusion and profusion of terms" (Macridis 1967, 20). However, each work takes a common view of party structure. The common thread that runs through much of this work is that the party is viewed as an institution with structures that guide the actions of its participants.

From Michels's oligarchic structures to Cotter and his colleagues' "bureaucratic party organization," the party is believed to possess certain structural attributes without which it ceases to be a party at all. This understanding of the party has created numerous conceptions of what constitutes the party's institution. Each of these various perspectives on political parties usually begins with an institutional benchmark, ranging from bureaucratic apparatus to machine-style structures, which draws into its orbit all of those things relevant to party activity.

Though each often has a different starting point, the net effect is that parties are understood to exhibit certain institutional characteristics that then account for the party's capacity to carry out a host of critical tasks such as the recruitment of candidates for office, the mobilization of voters, and the concentration of power in the formal institutions of the government.

Early studies of political parties primarily stressed their structural properties, emphasizing the place of the activist and leadership core within it. The first generation of studies sensitive to this aspect of the parties was generally written by European scholars. Political parties of the nineteenth and early twentieth-century were viewed as too strong and influential, and since the institution was often fueled by patronage, too corrupt. This was the political party that James Bryce (1959) criticized in *The American Commonwealth*.

Another critic of both American and British parties was Ostrogorski (1921). While acknowledging the necessary place of parties in modern democracies, he nevertheless criticized them for their excesses. Ostrogorski was especially disturbed by the permanent nature of political parties and their ability to command long-term loyalties that he viewed as dysfunctional and that ultimately interfered with the process of representation. He favored single-issue groups that would mobilize voters, and then dissolve when the issue had passed.

After the works of Bryce and Ostrogorski, American scholars generally took a more favorable view of parties, especially the urban machines. The most notable are the works of Harold Gosnell (1937), Frank Kent (1923), Roy Peel (1935), and John T. Salter (1935) all paying particular attention to the participants in the party's structure.

The most thorough treatments of party structure can be found in the works of Robert Michels (1949), Maurice Duverger (1954), and Samuel Eldersveld (1962).

Robert Michels, in his analysis of the German Socialist Democratic party, first posed the question of the relationship of the party structure to the party system. Michels's answer to the question was to conclude that "power is always conservative" and that within a party institution "the struggle for great principles becomes impossible" (1949, 366). Michels's developed the "Iron Law of Oligarchy"—"who says organization, say oligarchy" (1949, 32) According to Michels, the party gradually develops a leadership group as the organization increases in size. This leadership becomes increasingly professional and specialized, thus insulated from its support base. This growing gap between leaders and followers eventually culminates in the development of a cohesive elite whose primary incentive is to stay in power. They evolve into a self-perpetuating elite because they, as institutional leaders, control information and recruitment of new elites. Organizational development, he argues, necessarily results in a new political class. New elites who do not threaten the interests of the established elite cadre are absorbed.

Party theorists since Michels have reacted to the "conspiratorial" aspect of the oligarchical elite by emphasizing the historical development and circumstances in which parties organize.

Maurice Duverger (1954) took issue with Michels's "Iron Law of Oligarchy" by proposing a distinction between the cadre structure (consisting of a set of leaders or notables active only at election time) and the mass party structure (consisting of leaders and party members or adherents interacting in an ongoing institution in pursuit of common ends). While American parties were characterized as "cadre," the socialist mass membership parties represented the modern party of the future.

The important contribution that Duverger made to the party organization literature is the development of the idea that party is "a community with a particular structure." Contemporary parties "are characterized by their anatomy" (1954, xv). Duverger comes close to arguing that structure is the most important consideration in party research, and proceeds from the assumption that these institutional characteristics provide a basis for comparative study.

American scholars found Duverger's description of American parties as cadre in structure as a useful one. However, Duverger's resolution of Michels's elite "conspiracy" resulted in an unflattering characterization of the American party system as not typifying a modern society. Leon Epstein (1967) claims that "American parties, so often regarded as underdeveloped by European standards, are really responses to American conditions which cannot, in their entirety, be regarded as marks of a backward nation supposed to eventually resemble Europe" (Epstein 1967, 6). In contrast to Duverger, Epstein analyzed parties not from their structural development and complexity, but from the functions they fulfill. In doing so, Epstein provided a theoretical focus that shifted the concept of the party away from a structural emphasis. There is no structural imperative—the more developed party, for Epstein, is not necessarily the more modern. For Epstein, the cadre party developed from "parties with primarily and almost entirely an electoral function" (1967, 99). Mass membership parties began not as parties, but as social movements—"a pre-modern class consciousness, a delayed mass voting franchise, and widespread economic deprivation" (Epstein 1967 165).

Eldersveld's study of Detroit area precinct committee members provided another important condemnation of Michels's theory. Eldersveld attacked the concept of the oligarchic elite on two fronts. First, the institutional structure of American parties is not hierarchical. It is instead, stratarchical, based on a "reciprocal deference structure" (1964, 9). The basis of the leadership was rapport, not expertise. The leadership is sensitive to local interests and culture. Contrary to authoritarian or bureaucratic models of organization, the "critical action locus of the party is at its base" (1964, 9).

Second, the party comprises diverse elites with different career patterns, not a single unified elite. This pluralism derives from the quixotic nature of the party leaders' authority and the high level of turnover among party personnel. Turnover can result in the loss of power, or in a reconstitution of the party's subcoalitions. The party is a "social group," uniting "an agglomeration of people with a rich variety of motivations, drives, and needs" (1964, 303).

While Eldersveld himself contributed to a party theory of organization, the thrust of his research was to initiate a focus on the variety of institutional incentives and commitments between leaders and activists. Eldersveld emphasizes the behavior that flows from the unique structure of political parties.

Organizational theorists with their analysis of incentives for organization, had long considered the political party a special case of group organization, subject to the same dynamics as other organized groups (e.g., Wilson 1973; Olson 1965). Mancur Olson (1965) pointed out the limitations of large groups with latent interests: "Only when groups are small, or when they are fortunate enough to have an independent set of selective incentives, will they organize or act to achieve their objectives" (1965, 167). Political parties, organized for collective ends, are at a disadvantage in the capacity for organization. Therefore, beyond the individual benefits of office holding, and selective incentives provided by the party (for example, patronage), the logic of collective action is such that a party organization will remain weak. Large groups will always be at a disadvantage compared to the strong organization of primary or intermediate groups.

A similar argument has been advanced by James Q. Wilson (1973). In an early work, Peter Clark and James Q. Wilson argued that "all viable organizations must provide tangible or intangible incentives to individuals in exchange for contributions of individual activity" (1961, 130). They argued that incentive systems are central to understanding the dynamics of organizational change. "The distribution of motives through the society defines the potential contributors to various organizations. As motives change, so too will organizations. Some organizations will grow or decline spontaneously as the particular incentives they offer become relatively more or less appealing. . . ." (1961, 164). They submit the decline of the political party machine as an illustration of the effect of the decline of material incentives for activism.

James Q. Wilson's analysis of the Democratic clubs in three cities in the 1950s illustrates how these incentive systems are useful in analyzing party change. In *The Amateur Democrat*, he identified a new style among party activists. There was an influx of those who believed that the party should be "programmatic, internally democratic, and largely or entirely free of reliance on material incentives such as patronage" (1962, 340). Material incentives had declined, and this left only purposive and solidary incentives to motivate activism. Thus, the emergence of candidate followings represents an intermediate type of organization. According to Wilson, "In many of these organizations, the candidate himself and his chief aides still are attracted to politics as a vocation: if successful they will win paying jobs, while their followers must be content with either the fun of the game, the sense of victory, or devotion to the cause" (1973, 115).

The study of the institutional basis of the party has been ignored in recent scholarship, despite the fact that "the great theoretical tradition in the study of political parties was established by men with a distinctly organizational approach to the study of parties" (Sorauf 1967, 36). Sorauf said one reason for this neglect lies in what he calls the "Law of Available Data." Evidence for this can be found in the number of studies that have examined state or national delegates to nominating conventions (Rapoport et al. 1986; Kirkpatrick 1976; Miller and Jennings 1986). The thrust of this research has been the study of the attitudes of the newer party activists. Jeane Kirkpatrick (1976) surveyed delegates to determine their organizational style, with the assumption that changes in the delegate composition would yield clues about the parties' structure. Miller and Jennings (1986) extend this line of inquiry by analyzing delegates' attachment to the parties and attitude proximity to the public. They conclude that ideological goals (or purposive incentives) were insufficient incentives for organizational maintenance, compared to the self-interest considered the norm among party elites. Thus, it was assumed that the values of the new elites were "predictive of the future of the party organization, since the convention delegates of today are taken to be the organizational leaders of the future" (Cotter et al. 1984, 143). Hence, the delegate studies extend research adapted from voting behavior research, while the study of party as an institution declined.

In an attempt to shift the focus back to the structure of political parties, Cotter and his colleagues (1984) gathered direct information on various facets of party organization at the state and local levels. Their concern is that, before we can draw conclusions about the party system as a whole, we must understand what has been happening to parties as institutions over the last several decades.

For them, strong parties require both "organizational complexity and programmatic capacity," and both together imply a certain level of bureaucratization (Gibson et al. 1983, 198). They conclude that state and local parties have not only been persisting, but they have increased in strength, primarily because parties are becoming more bureaucratized.

Furthermore, in their conception of party institutional strength, they attempt to distinguish between the "elements of party *organization*, as distinct from party *activity*" (Gibson et al. 1985, 146). They lament the almost exclusive focus on the party's activities, at the expense of an understanding of the party's structure. They propose instead that we should use the structure of the party as a gauge for measuring party organizational strength.

However, the "structure" that they have in mind is a bureaucracy, and this sets a narrow limit on the party's boundaries. There is no reason to believe that a bureaucratically structured party is a necessary condition to parties engaging in electoral or programmatic activity, even high levels of activity. Additionally, this approach automatically equates a party bureaucracy with party institutional strength, but there is nothing automatic about it. An elaborate party bureaucracy is not effective if it is poorly integrated with the other facets of the party. Viable political parties are more than just permanent headquarters, professional staffs, and high-tech workshops. Without meaningful linkage with voters and office holders, the bureaucracy means very little. Generalizations about the condition of the party should not be made by simply seeing whether the party's structure adheres to a bureaucratic-style of organization.

Joseph Schlesinger's recent work (1985) is also an attempt to deal with the apparent paradox between the resurgence of certain party structures with the continuing electoral disaggregation. He borrows from the "office seeking" approach and expands the Downsian notion of teams of candidates who seek to control government by winning office to encompass those party workers recruited to assist in seeking voters' support. Thus, one would expect an increase in organizational cooperation in campaigns among party nuclei.

Schlesinger takes Downs's definition a step further to develop a theory of party organization (1965; 1984). He argues that the basic unit of the party is the collective effort of a candidate and his followers to capture a single public office. This is the nuclear party organization, and it is the basic building block of the party's structure. More complex structures emerge when candidates and incumbents unite their efforts to attain political office. Schlesinger excludes voters from his definition to recapture "the reality of the party" (1984, 377). E. E. Schattschneider similarly conceptualized parties by arguing that "whatever else the parties may be, they are not associations of the voters who support the party candidates" (1942, 53).

In his theory, Schlesinger argues that the separatist tendencies in the party system have resulted in increased cooperation among party nuclei. Congressional and party reform, an increase in primaries, expansion of the electorate, and the end of malapportioned districts have increased flexibility in the electorate and have increased party competition.

One criticism of Schlesinger's view of parties is that is more closely resembles a theory of "campaign organizations," rather than "party organizations" (Cotter et al. 1984, 2). It is true that Schlesinger's primary focus is on the electoral phase, however, the extent to which these cooperative links exist in other spheres of the party's activity goes beyond a view of the party as simply a super campaign apparatus. In some areas and for some candidates this may indeed constitute the extent of party activity—a candidate and a group of campaign workers bound by the efforts to win a single political office. However, Schlesinger's approach does not preclude the existence of a more complex arrangement between the party elite.

Another benefit of Schlesinger's approach is that it draws us away from the expectation that political parties possess a predetermined set of institutional attributes. The focus is on activity rather than structure, on coordinated linkages between party elite rather than formally-defined ties. The effect is to expand the possibilities for new forms of organization: the incorporation of new techniques and participants within the party sphere. If those activities fulfill certain vital functions important to the survival of the parties, the actual structural characteristics of the parties are irrelevant. This notion echoes E. E. Schattschneider's ideas on party organization:

> The problem of party organization is so different from that of smaller associations that it is often misunderstood. Parties are usually compared with smaller organizations, nearly always to the disadvantage of the parties, but parties cannot be judged by the standards used to measure other organizations. (1960, 58–59)

What standards, then, should we use? This question extends beyond the problem of attempting to measure party strength; that would require agreement on what a political party is, but clearly there is no consensus. The problem really is whether political parties are organizations at all, and, if so, what type.

THE MEANING OF ORGANIZATION

Political parties are said to have, or are thought to be, organizations, yet there is little discussion about what this means. Nothing written here will provide a definitive answer to this question; my aim is to explore the usefulness of the organization idea as a tool for understanding the parties. Organizations are often conceived in different ways, thus adding to our confusion about the "organizational basis" of the party.

On the one hand, political parties are called organizations because they unite a wide range of individuals under a party label with a clear partisan purpose: to win elections. On the other hand, parties are considered organizations because they exhibit permanent institutional features such as a party head-quarters, permanent staff, and other bureaucratic characteristics. The problem is that "organization" is used to mean different things and gives us little leverage on the structural basis of the party. When scholars point to the decline or resurgence of political parties, which concept of organization are they referring to? Often it is unclear. Do they mean the inability of parties to carry out its electoral activities or are they referring to the disappearance of the institutional aspects of the party with which we have become accustomed?

The problem is further complicated because the "organizational" attributes of the party are often listed without any reference to their consequences. Concepts of organizational strength, effectiveness, and complexity have no meaning for political parties beyond an electoral test. Many party scholars measuring the party's institutional attributes proceed from the belief that parties need only exhibit certain institutional features to be considered effective (such as bureaucratic ones) without linking those attributes to any consequences for the party. What institutional features are important and why are they important?

Approaches to the study of party organization emphasize two different ideas. The first attempts to distinguish between the various types of party institutions, viewing the party as a structure that draws into its orbit large numbers of voters, candidates, and party workers. The second approach largely sees parties in terms of activities they perform. Proponents of this approach frequently identify parties with campaigns. The distinction is crucial. Observers following the first approach view the activities performed by parties as a consequence flowing from a particular institutional configuration. Hence, parties require specific structural attributes to engage in certain activities. Party theorists using the second approach do not believe that parties must adhere to a stipulated structural pattern. Thus, a party is an institutional response to the necessity of engaging in certain activities or tasks, such as the mobilization of electoral support. This institution varies from setting to setting as environmental conditions change.

One fundamental problem with using the first approach is that it raises the possibility that changes in the structural basis of the party will go unde-tected as it adapts to new environmental conditions. New party forms may emerge that do not correspond to the institutional benchmark set by the researcher. It is not the commitment to a particular structure that charac-terizes the political party, but the activity that flows from it. For example, state laws have created a complex array of party offices at the local, county, and state levels, and traditional efforts to study parties, especially at the state and local level, have concentrated on this formal apparatus. But this was never the "real" party. The legally-defined apparatus was a tool used by reformers in the late-nineteenth and early-twentieth centuries who were frustrated in their attempts to curb the power of the machines. It was a legal requirement *imposed* on a party that already existed.

This points to a weakness in traditional efforts to study party organizations. The degree to which these positions influence the nominating phase, the running of campaigns, or affect the government process differs widely from one state to another (Jewell and Olson 1982, 112–120). Moreover, studying this formal apparatus tells us very little about how the party performs a variety of tasks—how it grooms candidates for office, how the party finances its campaign efforts, or how the party orchestrates its activity in the electoral and governmental phases.

This emphasis on the formal party apparatus stems, in part, from a preoccupation with the more overt and conspicuous aspects of the party's structure. This has lead many party scholars to make misleading generalizations about the nature of political parties. They contend that few of the party offices at the state and local level have a sustained leadership, and few wield significant power. Where statutes ordain (and political scientists expect) active legions of party workers and layer upon layer of vigorous organization, there is often only sporadic activity by a handful of transient party officials. Furthermore, these poorly articulated (from a bureaucratic point of view) party structures have led to pessimistic conclusions about the effectiveness of the party to perform various functions in the political system.

It is, therefore, not surprising that many scholars insist that most state and local parties have ineffective and empty organizations, looking impressive on paper, but wielding little power. However, rather than declaring that modern parties lack effective organizations, we should instead reevaluate the usefulness of the concept of organization as a tool for studying the parties.

UNITING ACTIVITIES AND STRUCTURE

Earlier I presented a definition of the party that emphasized the institutional basis of the party as the deliberate coordination of activity aimed at the capture of public office. The institutional components of the party should be sought in terms of this activity, whether formally prescribed or not, rather than through the identification of formal party structures.

Cotter et al. (1984) proceed from the conviction that the party should be sought in terms of its structure, rather than the activities that it performs. My perspective is just the opposite: the party should be sought in terms of the activities it performs, using this as a guide to its structure. This approach is rooted in the idea that the party's structure is a response to a variable set of constraints imposed by the need for parties to parallel the complex structures of government and adapt to a variety of political and social settings. Despite the differences in these constraints by location, the parties display a remarkable capacity to perform the activities necessary to their survival in the political system. Insisting that parties adhere to some predetermined structure, especially a bureaucratic one, limits the possibility of identifying alternative methods for achieving similar results, for performing the same tasks.

This restores party activity as a central variable in the study of political parties. The "organizational" approach to the study of parties unfortunately creates an unnecessary set of requirements for political parties. How parties are structured becomes more important than what they do. It is important to realize that the structural properties of political parties are an institutional *response* to the need to carry out certain activities. As conditions change, so too will the response. The need to perform certain activities, on the other hand, remains constant. No matter how they are structured, institutions that contest elections, recruit candidates for office, and exercise power in government to satisfy their supporters are political parties. The only legitimate test, then, is to evaluate how well these tasks are accomplished. We need to move away from approaches that emphasize the institutionalization or formalization of party ties and structures, the hallmarks of the traditional organizational approach.

At one level, this conceptualization leads to the conclusion that the American party is a loosely structured system of actors and activities. In reality, political parties are not "organizations" at all, at least in the way that we traditionally define them. This does not mean, however, that political parties in America lack structure. It simply means that comparing political parties to other organizations and using "organizational" theories will yield little understanding on the nature of political parties in the United States. At some time and in some places, political parties in America may have resembled organizations, but it is not a requisite component. The lack of formal party structures does not necessarily point to any defect in American political parties. They simply did not require the kinds of structures found in other European settings; those structures were never necessary (see also Aldrich 1995).

The idea that the party can be conceived as an informal institution departs from the traditional view that the parties are synonymous with their formal apparatus. However, this is a particularly useful, and possibly superior, approach to studying the party because it does not discard the party's formal structure; it simply demands that, to be considered a significant component of the party, it must engage in certain critical activities like candidate recruitment, electoral activity, or coordination of power within government. As Robert Merton wrote concerning the urban machines,

> . . . the functional deficiencies of the official structure generate an alternative (unofficial) structure to fulfill existing needs somewhat more effectively. (1957, 82)

These topics receive full attention in the chapters that follow, for they are important to a proper understanding of the development of parties in the United States. Ultimately, any conclusion concerning the existence of parties is dependent on how the term "party" is understood. In the end, many of the differences between political scientists can be attributed to different definitions.

3

The Party Web

The reports of my death are greatly exaggerated.
—Samuel Clemens, 1897

To know where American parties may be heading, it is necessary to know where they have been. The major trends that emerge from the past often have a profound and lasting impact upon the present and the future. As an increasing number of immigrants began to arrive from foreign shores during the middle and the latter nineteenth-century, the nature of municipal politics in America underwent a dramatic transformation. Since authority was so dispersed in the formal structures of government, political leaders relied on an informal, extralegal institution, usually a political party, for centralizing or concentrating influence. At the head of the party was the "boss" who sat at the top of an informal, hierarchical institution that encompassed elected officials, government employees, district or ward leaders, and precinct workers. This was the urban political machine that captured the imagination of reformers, journalists, and academics for a century or more.

But, since then, many have argued that change in elections and in government over the last century have inexorably eroded the strength of the urban machine. According to this viewpoint, civil service reforms, the institution of the Australian ballot, the expansion of direct primaries, and the emergence of electronic media have not only dismantled the urban machines, but they have also worked against the long-term survival of parties throughout the country. In this new environment, the parties' candidates can directly communicate with voters without depending on the party to make it on the ballot or to mobilize the vote. Some even argue that political parties have become a throwback to another era.

However tempting this conclusion may be, there is, in reality, little evidence one way or the other concerning how these changes have affected the parties. Notwithstanding the disappearance of the urban machines as they functioned in the nineteenth-century, there has been scant research on how parties have responded to changes in elections and government. Most often,

33

scholars have simply assumed that certain reforms or changes would greatly affect party development without providing much in the way of evidence (Pomper 1977; Polsby 1983; Crotty and Jacobson 1980). The party is often portrayed as powerless to respond to this changing environment. But this is an unreasonable assumption. Political parties have always been adaptive institutions. Their emergence in a variety of political settings throughout the world is testimony to their adaptability.

This chapter examines the model or benchmark that most party scholars use when evaluating the contemporary parties, that is, parties from nineteenth-century America—the Golden Age of Politics. Throughout the chapter, I refer to this as the old party and the contemporary party as the new party.

Our assessments of contemporary parties are unfortunately tainted by a conception of the strength and effectiveness of political parties from this era. When evaluating the new party, many political scientists judge contemporary parties weak because they implicitly or explicitly hold contemporary parties to a standard a century old. Regrettably, this has limited our sensitivity to the different ways parties have adapted to a novel set of conditions. Contemporary assessments of the new party are often laced with a nostalgia for parties from the Golden Age. In addition, many accounts of the old party exaggerate its strength. The extent to which this party form was typical of American politi-cal parties is also unclear. We must, therefore, hold contemporary parties to a more realistic standard, one which incorporates a more balanced evaluation of the impact that changes in elections and government have had on party development.

It is unrealistic to expect parties to possess the same institutional features as parties more than a century old. Not only should we adjust our expecta-tions about the institutional basis of the contemporary party, but we should also reexamine the different ways we judge party effectiveness. The social and political environment of the nineteenth-century produced one institu-tional expression of the party and these factors give rise to quite another one today. To expect contemporary parties to adhere to a particular set of struc-tural features misses what we should be looking for in political parties.

That the institutional basis of the parties has changed is irrelevant to the question of party effectiveness. In contrast, judging the parties on what they do directly impinges on one's assessment of the strength of the parties. The parties of the nineteenth-century possessed an effective institutional framework that accomplished a variety of ends, which arguably made them "strong" par-ties. The parties of today possess a different institutional framework aimed at accomplishing the same ends. We must, therefore, judge what parties do, rather than how they are structured; evaluate them by results of the structure that they do possess instead of inspecting the congruence between the old and the new institutional forms. To argue otherwise is to suggest that the party has only one kind of institution that gives rise to a particular level of effectiveness. It is just as plausible to argue that effectiveness can be achieved through other means.

Before we consider what makes for effective parties, it may be instructive to specify the standard that is often used as a starting point for the study of American political party organizations.

PARTIES IN THE GOLDEN AGE: THE PARTY BENCHMARK

We are told that the American parties of the nineteenth-century enjoyed wide support among voters; they effectively controlled office holders; they recruited and groomed candidates for office; and nineteenth-century party workers insured that their partisans made it to the polls. Many accounts of the old party give vivid details of nineteenth-century politics, where party extravaganzas were diversions from the struggles of day-to-day life (Tocqueville 1945; Bryce 1959). Party-sponsored gatherings were a feature of both city and country life. In the cities, they resembled street carnivals, and in rural areas, farmers came from miles around to listen to political oratory at a fairground. In this age, political parties could depend on the fervent partisanship of their voters, rooted in social and religious issues such as prohibition, nativism, and slavery. The local and state party committees raised campaign funds to subsidize a partisan press and to print and distribute literature carrying their message to the voters.

It is also said that, unlike the parties of today, the old party maintained personal contact with voters; it actively pursued voter support through clear positions on the issues; and it maintained a complex party apparatus that extended through all levels of government and society. Some view this as the Golden Age in American politics: turnout was high and voters were aware of the issues (Burnham 1970). Many scholars have presented a long list of activities—such as the recruitment of candidates, the mobilization of voters, and the development of a system that sustains a stable workforce—that the parties used to perform, which have since atrophied (e.g., Pomper 1977). Hence, the parties are either dead or not far from it. All seem to unanimously agree that parties, as institutions, were stronger then than they are today.

Given this image of the old party, many party observers are struck by how weak contemporary parties appear to be, standing in stark contrast to their predecessors. In contemporary parties, few of the party offices at the state and local level have a sustained leadership, and few party offices wield significant power. Some areas still support party machines, but these are merely pale replicas of their nineteenth-century counterparts.

Although well-oiled and effective party institutions did exist, they were neither as monolithic, nor as widespread, as conventional wisdom implies.

Much of the criticism of contemporary parties stems from comparing them
to this glorified standard. Most parties had to struggle to keep party positions
filled. Few state and local parties had a permanent headquarters, paid staff,
or even consistent campaign resources. In fact, the typical American party
"organization" was spartan in nature. No matter how complex those structures, they have rarely been based on a dues-paying membership commonly
found in other countries. In contrast to European mass membership parties,
American cadre parties were always institutionally spare. Skeletal organizations have been a dominant American form both before and since the Golden
Age of politics, and in many places during that Age (Sorauf 1984, 59–86).
Only in a few local areas did these institutions gain the renown of the famous
urban machine. And even in these instances, they rarely achieved the level of
effectiveness described by many contemporary party scholars.

Yet the political machines were the parties that the reformers reacted
against when they tried to regulate party activity. Since then, because some
political machines operated in visible government arenas, we persuaded our-
selves that they were the typical American party organization.

SHAKY GIANTS?

In Boss Tweed's New York, political power was quite fragmented (Erie
1988; Hershkowitz 1977, 144–148; Mushkat 1971, 379; Callow 1966, 107;
Mandelbaum 1965, 55; Myers 1917, 262). There was no single group or
organization that controlled the city, or for that matter, the party. Rather, it
was a party made up of many confrontational elites and competing political
cliques. Ward leaders, who are often depicted by contemporary descriptions
as the party's foot-soldiers, faithfully obeying orders that came down through
the chain of command from the boss, were also the party's leading source of
opposition (Callow 1966, 107; Stoddard 1931, 107). In fact, the leadership
of Tammany could not organize a slate for offices elected by ward or district
constituencies (Mandelbaum 1958, 65). Unable to command their obedience,
Tweed had to purchase the support of other politicians on an ad hoc,
individual-by-individual basis. For example, Tweed was only able to secure
passage of the city charter of 1870 by distributing bribes to both Tammany
and Republican legislators (Callow 1966, 229).

Many of the problems that plagued Tweed also plagued the man that
followed him, John Kelly. From the mid-1870s to the end of the 1880s, competing factions divided the Democratic party in New York City. Two factions
posed especially serious threats to Tammany's hegemony during this period,
the Irving Hall Democracy and the New York County Democracy. These factions were as successful as Tammany in electing their candidates to the Board

of Aldermen, the mayoralty, and to lesser city offices. They even gained the recognition of the state party apparatus. Between 1880 and 1888, 65 of the 114 Democrats who were elected to the Board of Aldermen were either members of the Irving Hall Democracy or New York County Democracy (Brown and Smith 1922).

Tammany's leadership during this period also faced problems in controlling the behavior of their nominal followers in office. Tammany aldermen and state legislators were not disciplined troops. Rather, they would form pacts in which they agreed to sell their votes as units to the highest bidder. Tammany's own deputies on the Board of Aldermen granted the franchise for a street railway in return for a cash bribe of $500,000 (Hirsch 1948).

The history of the Tammany machine is filled with episodes in which ward leaders would break with the boss and establish their own group (Callow 1966, 111–112). In many such cases, these insurgents were unsuccessful against a well-organized party, but in many others, these insurgents formed splinter groups that eventually wrested control of city government away from the machine. Revolts against the leadership were common under normal circumstances, and during tumultuous times, the organization was thrown into chaos. Insurgent candidates would disrupt party conventions, defying the party boss. And the leadership of Tammany itself revolved from one faction to another (Mushkat 1971, 366-367). Such histories leave open to question the extent to which the party actually controlled its candidates, who often had loyal followings of their own.

Besides the problems of disciplining its own politicians, Tammany was also plagued by problems from below. Working-class voters often supported labor parties instead of the machine. Steven Erie suggests that, as opposed to conventional wisdom, the political machines did not command a vast supply of patronage (1988, 6–7, 29). In fact, it was the lack of enough patronage to satisfy all the different groups that spurred many of the revolts against the machine's leadership. The traditional view is that the machines were toppled by middle-class reformers who became incensed with the excesses of the machines and their bosses. But the threat from working-class immigrants was at least as great, and these groups proved to be a constant source of instability, often pulling down the machines because they felt they were not getting a fair share of the municipal spoils. The large influx of new immigrants put a strain on the machine's management of constituent demands, and many did not survive in this unstable environment (Erie 1988, 53–57). The machines were caught between a rock and a hard place. One the one hand, the working-class voters were threatening rebellion because they were not getting enough patronage, and on the other hand, middle-class voters were organizing antimachine parties because they felt victimized by the high taxes that went to support the patronage.

For all of the celebrated efficacy of the Golden Age party, the political machine still needed and received votes from people who were not part of the organization. The conventional view is that the machine had an iron-grip on its constituents, but the reality is very different: never did Tammany control a majority of votes in the city (Callow 1966, 10). Many voters voted out of habit or longtime allegiance for the party, and Tammany relied on these voters to return them to office. The Tammany experience was hardly unique. Descriptions of party politics in Chicago, Cincinnati, San Francisco, Jersey City, New Orleans, Texas, and upstate New York all reveal party institutions struggling to keep power (Anders 1982; Connors 1971; Miller 1968; Bean 1967; Thomas 1962; Reynolds 1936; Gosnell 1924; Lewis 1901).

This was an age when the political machine was equipped with a patronage-based workforce that it could use during elections. The urban machine was furnished with a set of tools and was rooted in a society that enhanced the achievement of its electoral ends. In this setting, it was possible for the party to construct an institution that looked much like the Golden Age standard. However, several things stand out.

First, office holders were not powerless against the "regular" party. Accounts of the old party are filled with instances where elected officials defied the party. Office holders were often able to secure resources of their own to resist the party's leadership.

Second, besides internal difficulties, the old party was frequently chal-lenged from outside its institution. We have this image of an institution that was impervious to challenge—once in power the machine was there to stay. The reality is just the opposite. The machines constantly faced challenges from other organized groups and were, at times, thrown out of office.

Third, the fragmentation of power within the institution itself just does not match the image of the monolithic party described today. Shifting alliances, insurgent and independent-minded candidates, and disgruntled party regulars were a constant source of uncertainty.

The old party sometimes had access to sanctions with which it could enforce discipline. And the structure of the old party, fueled by the spoils of municipal government, was occasionally hierarchical. But the strength of nineteenth-century parties, especially *typical* American parties of that period, seldom live up to our romanticized images of the unimpeachable party boss and his efficient army of party workers. Much of the lamenting for the passing of the machines has a nostalgic tone about it, overestimating their prevalence as an American political form.

STRUCTURE AS A MEANS TO AN END

The notion that contemporary parties lack effective institutions stems from two different, but interrelated, arguments. The first suggests that parties have declined in importance because of the changes that have occurred in the electoral process. The institution of the Australian ballot, the widespread adoption of the direct primary, and the emergence and use of the new techniques for communicating with voters eroded the role of the party in the electoral arena.

The second argument suggests that other changes such as civil service reforms have eroded the institutional base of the party. The party no longer has the resources to maintain a stable and effective workforce to carry out many of the tasks crucial to the continued effectiveness of the party. Both factors are argued to have undermined the party's role in the political process.

According to this viewpoint, these factors acting independently or in combination have had three consequences for the modern party. The first was that the new party no longer had a pool of participants from which to draw candidates to represent the party in office. Furthermore, the inability to offer these candidates aid during elections has forced candidates to become more independent, divorcing their fate from that of the party. In the old party institution, after working on the party's behalf for years, party workers were groomed for office and selected to run with the party's blessing. The party's choices were meaningful because it had the machinery for getting the candidate's name on the ballot and for influencing the electoral process. Maverick and insurgent candidates were at a severe disadvantage against the party's chosen candidates. Even with the adoption of the direct primary, successful candidates were those who were the best organized, and this still often required the aid of the party to mobilize primary voters.

The second consequence is that the modern party has lost the means for insuring that a minimum of campaign tasks are carried out on election day. The contemporary party is hindered by a largely voluntaristic and transient party workforce. As civil service reforms began to limit the numbers of patronage workers that the party could use to fill vital party positions, the party's formal institutions were characterized by high turnover. A workforce supported by patronage provided a stable source of personnel that could be counted to perform the campaign chores necessary to insure the party's dominance in the electoral process.

Along with these changes that eroded the institutional base of the parties, changes in elections themselves have supposedly diminished the role of the party in the electoral process. The development and use of the different mass communication techniques, especially television, meant that candidates for public office did not require the party to communicate with its supporters.

Candidates for office and office holders could circumvent the party and establish their own core of technically skilled workers to appeal directly to the electorate. The party was unable to counteract these new methods of campaigning because it lacked even the old-fashioned core of participants to influence the electoral process. It is argued that the parties of today simply lack a cadre of party workers to insure a consistent and effective presence in the electoral process.

The third consequence was that the party had no effective means for insuring the cooperation of its candidates once in office, since they no longer held the key to their future electoral success. Control of nomination procedures and outcomes enabled the party to coordinate the efforts of its office holders in government. It is now argued that the party lacks the incentives to insure even the minimum degree of coordination in the governmental phase. Self-selected candidates are no longer beholden to the party for their electoral success, therefore eliminating the party's influence over them.

These standards are rooted in the tasks that parties perform in the political arena *not* in the structures they manifest. However, seldom examined is the idea that the parties may have adapted to these changes by adopting alternative methods for carrying out these same tasks. There is little doubt that, if we expect contemporary parties to use the same institutional forms for coordinating its efforts in the political process as the old party, then the modern party will come up short. The question should be asked in a different way: are the parties using alternative methods for accomplishing the same tasks?

We need to proceed from the idea that it is the tasks performed by parties that are crucial, not their structural basis. It is reasonable to argue that certain goals or ends of the party are made possible by the development of a particular institutional base, but it is not its structure that makes it an effective institution, rather it is the things the institution can achieve. To argue otherwise is to suggest that the structure of parties and their goals are inseparable. This is the view that certain electoral tasks or activities can be accomplished using only a single method. This probably takes the argument too far. There are a variety of ways to accomplish the same goal. If we insist that parties adhere to a structure suited to another environment, then we will continue to judge them weak. It is unreasonable to expect American parties in 1994 to use the same techniques as they did in 1894. The parties of the nineteenth century were faced with one configuration of social and political circumstances, and the parties of today with quite another.

Although machines have (in the traditional form) all but disappeared, in many respects, they are being replaced by the incumbent's enterprise-in-office. The enterprise-in-office draws within its orbit political aides working for the incumbent, campaign specialists, and those holding formal leadership positions within the party. At the heart of this system are the political staffs working for office holders at various levels of government. What has emerged is an elaborate party institution based on the interaction and collaboration of these enterprises-in-office.

THE PARTY AS A NATIONAL FRANCHISE: THE PROFESSIONALIZATION OF CONGRESS

As recently as the 1950s, Congress could be described as a part-time institution. Its members arrived in Washington on the train sometime in January and left in the summer. When Congress adjourned in July or August, these politicians had enough spare time to pursue a career in private life—to practice law, run a business, or, if they were farmers, bring in the crops at the end of the harvest season.

In contrast, since the 1960s, Congress has essentially been in session year-round. It recesses for a month in August and every other year suspends business a month before each national election, but the rest of the time it spent in session. This does not mean that a member of Congress spends all of his or her time in Washington. A member can return home virtually every weekend, which increasingly begins Friday and ends the following Monday. Time spent away from Washington is usually consumed with running for office—attending fund raisers, meeting with constituent groups, or attending local meetings. In the modern Congress, there is no opportunity to pursue a career in private life.

The way that members of Congress campaign for office has also changed. Before the 1950s, there were obvious constraints on the ability of a member of Congress to campaign effectively on his own, rather than with the party. One of these was the limited range of techniques for reaching voters. With the numbers of voters he faced, personal contacts and friends could not provide the extensive network of informants and workers that a party precinct organization could. In the absence of opinion polling, there was no guide as to the public mood. They were separated from him by hundreds or thousands of miles. The choice of strategies was limited by the remoteness of Washington from many congressional districts, and made the perpetual campaign impossible. Train or car journeys to the west coast took several days, and it was only after WWII that long-distance air service placed the continental United States within a few hours of the Capitol. In addition, Congress did not allocate funds for large staffs in the district. Many members of Congress in the 1950s did not maintain a full-time office in the district. However, since the 1950s, the growth in resources available to members of Congress for district liaison has been spectacular.

The last several decades have seen an explosion in the resources available to members of Congress. This trend has several roots. The first is the

Figure 3.1
Growth of Personal Staff for Members of the House, 1960–1998

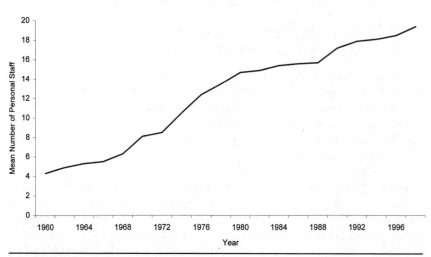

Source: Data compiled from the Congressional Staff Directory (Washington, D.C.: Congressional Staff Directory, Annual Editions, 1960–1999).

increase in the availability of staffs. Before the 1960s, members of Congress had limited resources to hire staff, so establishing district operations would weaken the Washington office. The growth of staffs accelerated during the 1960s and 1970s, making the deployment of staff to a district operation feasible. Also, the avalanche in citizen requests over the last several decades spurred the desire to handle the bulk of these requests in the district, freeing the Washington office to pursue legislative activities.

Figure 3.1 charts the growth in the mean number of personal staff assigned to members of Congress since 1960. Staff size has more than tripled, growing from an average size of less than five in 1960 to eighteen in 1999. Within memory of some congressional veterans, most replies to constituent mail were written by hand, and the only assistant that most legislators had was a clerk or secretary. A clerk was ordinarily a jack-of-all-trades who might answer the mail one moment and greet a visiting constituent the next. By the 1950s and the early 1960s, personal offices still had their share of clerks and secretaries, sometimes presided over by an administrative assistant.

The staff gains were modest during the 1960s. In 1964, for example, the average House member employed only six staffers, while Senators got by with fewer than twelve per office. Since the beginning of the 1970s, however, staff increases have been dramatic. Another way of looking at the growth

Table 3.1
Staff Allowances for Members of United States House

	Staff Allowance		Staff Allowance
1979	$288,156	1989	$431,760
1981	$336,384	1991	$475,000
1983	$336,648	1993	$557,400
1985	$394,680	1995	$568,560
1987	$406,560	1997	—[a]

Note: Since 1989, staff size was not to exceed twenty-two employees.
[a] Since 1995, three former expense allowances (staff, official expenses, and office mail) were combined into a memberís representational allowance. The members can spend the allowance as they see fit. In 1997, the mean allowance was $901,771.
Source: Ornstein, Mann, and Malbin (2000, 144–145).

over the last three decades is that today's House offices, with an average of eighteen employees, have far outstripped the average Senate office of the 1950s.

The Republican takeover of the House in 1995 produced dramatic changes in staff levels; however, this occurred primarily for committee, not personal, staff. Between 1993 and 1995, committee staff declined by a startling 70 percent, but personal staff declined by a mere 3 percent (Ornstein, Mann, and Malbin 2000).

With the increase in staff, members of Congress have also given themselves free travel to their districts, free mail, and free telephone services, and they have increased these allowances regularly. This change in the political resources of members of Congress has been important because it has made the constituency service of the individual public official more evident to the electorate. It can also be argued that the expansion of government services, fixed in the New Deal and then in the Great Society, has increased government contact with citizens, thereby increasing the number of potential clients for members of Congress-as-troubleshooters (Fiorina 1977).

By 1993, members of the House were entitled to a formidable array of resources. Including the member's own income, annual office salaries approach $500,000; added to this is a package of fringe benefits that increase the value of the package to $600,000. Beyond this, annual operating expenses, ranging from pencils to travel allowances home, average about $200,000. Moreover, the value of franking adds an additional $220,000 per House member (Ornstein, Mann, and Malbin, 2000). In 1995, the House GOP consolidated all of these expenses into a single account for each member. Table 3.1 details the increase in staff allowances for members of the House since 1979.

Crucial to understanding the congressional enterprise is the amount of control that legislators have in hiring, firing, and setting office policies. Although the House Administration Committee does enforce some limitations in certain areas, members have great flexibility in deciding how they will employ their considerable resources. For the most part, Congress has exempted itself from restrictive regulations, such as antidiscrimination statutes, which apply to the private sector.

Aides serve at the pleasure of the elected official, and the enterprise notion, which ties together the fortunes of members and their staffs, makes especially good sense in the day-to-day operations of the office.

The congressional enterprise-in-office has evolved into two distinct ways since the 1960s. First, staff growth has meant that the member could hire enough assistants to work in the district to provide a link between the individual member and the community. Much of this increase in staff resources has been devoted to establishing more elaborate district operations. Figures 3.2 and 3.3 trace the growth of district-based offices and the increase in the proportion of the staff deployed in the district.

In 1960, only 56 percent of members of Congress maintained a full-time district office, and those that did, generally kept a single person there to answer the phone and respond to some constituent mail. The bulk of the staff resided in Washington. By the mid-1970s, nearly all members of Congress had established a full-time district operation. Along with the surge in the number of members of Congress setting up district offices, there also has been a steady increase in the proportion of staff assigned in the district. In 1960, for those who maintained a full-time district office, members of Congress placed only 14 percent of their staff in the district. By 1999, nearly one-half of a member of Congress's staff could be found in the district.[1]

Second, and perhaps more importantly, staff duties began to change. The district office still handles the bulk of constituency requests; however, staffers are increasingly occupied with political work, including campaigns.

By the end of the 1970s, many legislators at the federal level retained aides who had campaign expertise so that they could deploy them in future elections. Aides from his or her first election campaign are often rewarded with employment as staffers. They might want the job for itself or, in some cases, to use the position as a stepping stone for their own careers. And those members of staff whom he wanted to work on his next election could then take a leave of absence from their government job, and could be reassigned to paid positions in the campaign organization.

Staff positions not only permitted members of Congress to retain campaign aides from one election to the next, but these district aides could also be lent to other candidates seeking office. This is a form of patronage politics that differs from the traditional form in one main respect. Incumbents, not the local party apparatus, now controlled the resources.

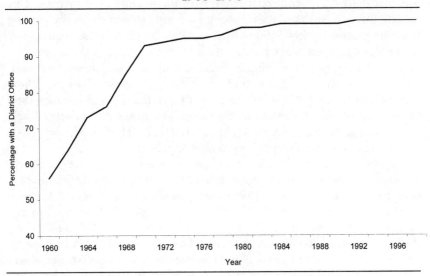

Figure 3.2
Percentage of Members of Congress's With Full-Time District Offices,
1960–1998

Source: Data compiled from the Congressional Staff Directory (Washington, D.C.:
Congressional Staff Directory, Annual Editions, 1960–1999).

Figure 3.3
Percentage of Members of Congress's Staff in the District, 1960–1998

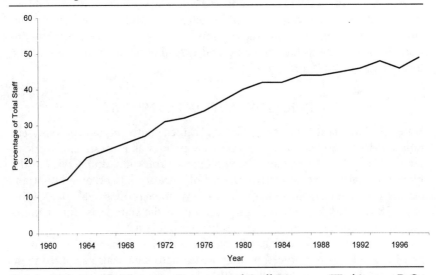

Source: Data compiled from the Congressional Staff Directory (Washington, D.C.:
Congressional Staff Directory, Annual Editions, 1960–1999).

Another fundamental change in Congress is the increasingly significant role that individual members are playing in the funding of campaigns. This redistribution of wealth is made possible by campaign war chests overflowing with spare cash—nearly $100 million as 1990 ended. With so many funds accumulated, members of Congress are more than willing to make contributions to the campaigns of other politicians, both within Congress and back home in the district. This is encouraged by federal election laws that allow members to operate PACs that increase their influence and advance their careers. Incumbents doled out nearly 4.3 million in the 1990 election cycle to House and Senate candidates. (Alston 1991). By 1998, leadership PACs contributed over 10 million dollars to other candidates (FEC 1998).

Parties leaders in the House and the Senate were especially active in accumulating surplus campaign funds in their own PACs, to distribute them later to other candidates. In 1998, for example, Dick Armey's *Majority Leader's Fund* contributed $879,892, Richard Gephart's *Effective Government Committee* donated $365,568, and Newt Gingrich's *Monday Morning PAC* contributed $765,500 to other candidates in need (FEC 1998). Creating your own PAC is one technique used by members of Congress, but others have simply doled out money from their own campaign war chest. For example, California congressmen Henry Waxman, Howard Berman, and Mel Levine, contributed $50,000, $42,000, and $36,000 respectively to other candidates out of their own funds. Henry Waxman also donated $152,000 from one of his affiliated PACs (Alston 1991).

The growth of congressional resources should make clear that democratization on Capitol Hill does not rest solely upon rules and procedures. Rather, all members can use their resources to insulate themselves from electoral uncertainty or bring those resources to bear in other electoral contests, thus advancing their influence and extending their power beyond the legislative entity in Washington.

THE QUIET REVOLUTION IN THE STATES

State legislatures are becoming like the United States House of Representatives. Most members of the House view politics as a career and work to retain their office. "As politics has become a profession, and service in the House a realistic and attractive career, job security has become important for the professional representative as for any other professional. . . ." (Cain et al. 1987, 7). Like Congress, once serving in the state legislature became attractive, incumbents sought to solidify their hold on it.

Just as members of Congress have acquired staff assistance, franking privileges, and district offices, many state legislators have also acquired these resources. To be sure, not all state legislators were in this position in the

Table 3.2
Total Staff in State Legislatures, 1979 to 1996

	Full-Time			Session Only[a]			Grand Total
	Professional	Clerical	Total	Professional	Clerical	Total	Total
1979	8,346	8,584	16,930	NA	NA	10,062	26,992
1988	13,755	10,814	24,569	1,268	7,559	8,827	33,396
1996	14,935	11,965	26,900	868	7,149	8,017	34,917
Percentage Change 1979 to 1996	79	39	59	—	—	–20	29

[a] These are staffers assigned to legislators for the legislative session only.
Source: National Conference of State Legislatures, 1998.

1970s. In some less populous states, the legislatures still meet every other year for a couple of months. For example, in states such as Vermont, the offices are still part-time and legislative salaries are small. It is possible to combine legislative service in Vermont with a career in private life—in fact, it is necessary. In many wealthier and industrialized states, legislatures have become fully professionalized. This made the job more attractive and provided the office holder with independent political resources (Jewell 1982). In 1998, thirty-seven state legislatures held regular sessions that lasted one hundred days or more, and most of those stayed in business half the year (National Conference of State Legislatures 1998). Nine state legislatures met more or less year-round. Today, in many states, there is little practical difference between being a member of a state legislature and Congress.

Like Congress, many states have also experienced large expansion in their staff system. Between 1979 and 1996, nearly 8,000 staffers were added to the nation's state legislatures (Table 3.2). This increase of almost 29 percent is fairly dramatic. More interesting is the apparent shift away from session staff and the phenomenal expansion of full-time professional staff that has occurred during this period.

In 1979, session staff represented over 37 percent of total legislative employees. By 1996, that figure had dropped to about 23 percent. In view of lengthier sessions in many states, this development may not be surprising. Many session employees very likely have been converted to full-time.

Table 3.3
Largest Staffs in 1979 with 1996 Comparison

1979 Ranking	1979 Total Staff	1996 Total Staff	% Change
1. New York	3,100	3,899	26
2. California	1,760	2,610	48
3. Texas	1,486	2,420	63
4. Pennsylvania	1,430	2,702	89
5. Florida	1,335	2,173	63
6. Illinois	1,119	1,057	–6
7. Michigan	1,047	1,357	30
8. Washington	920	902	–2
9. Oregon	663	484	–27
10. New Jersey	582	1,514	160
Total	13,442	19,118	42

Source: National Conference of State Legislatures, 1998.

Table 3.2 also shows that when legislatures have added staff, they most likely have added full-time professional staff. During this seventeen-year period, this category of legislative employees grew by over 6,500, or almost 80 percent. The growth of full-time professional staff represents nearly 85 percent of staff growth since 1979. Clearly, state legislatures are becoming more professional.

Table 3.3 lists the ten states with the largest staffs in 1979. Except for Oregon, all of these states have remained in the top ten since 1979. While the average change in staff for the nation is 24 percent, these states' staffs were 42 percent larger than in 1979. Perhaps even more significant, these ten states contributed over 5,676 of the 7,925 added in all the fifty states between 1979 and 1996.

The ten largest staffs in 1979 together represented 50 percent of all state legislative staff in the country. In 1996, with New Jersey joining the top ten, that figure has grown to over 160 percent. While states with large staffs set the pace for expansion, the smallest ten legislative staffs in 1979 had not added many employees by 1996 (Table 3.4).

The ten smallest staffs in 1979 together represented just over 5 percent of all state legislative staff in the country. By 1996, with Nevada leaving the bottom ten and Mississippi joining, that percentage had dropped to 5.2 percent. On average, the ten smallest states grew by 32 percent, although Nevada and Delaware showed significant percentage increases.

Generally speaking, the states with large staffs are heavily populated states with large urban centers and competitive political climates. They have

Table 3.4
Smallest Staffs in 1979 with 1996 Comparison

1979 Ranking	1979 Total Staff	1996 Total Staff	% Change
1. Vermont	65	58	−11
2. Wyoming	98	125	28
3. Delaware	107	164	53
4. North Dakota	126	172	37
5. South Dakota	135	94	−30
6. New Hampshire	140	159	14
7. Maine	154	180	17
8. Idaho	175	158	−10
9. Utah	182	225	24
10. Nevada	205	490	139
Total	1,387	1,825	32

Source: National Conference of State Legislatures, 1998.

decentralized staff organizations and provide relatively generous personal staff resources to members (Weberg 1988, 192). Most of these states have full-time professional legislatures. In contrast, the smaller states are more rural and are more dominated by one party. In small states, the staff organizations are highly centralized with few personal staff resources available to members.

Beyond the sheer growth in staff, another change is altering the way many states do business: the shift from nonpartisan staffs to personal and partisan staffs. Today, the fastest growing category of legislative staffers is those assigned to the party caucuses or to individual legislators. Since the mid-1960s, partisan staff in Wisconsin has tripled, growing from twenty to a total of sixty staffers. In Illinois, the size of the partisan staff has quadrupled, so that today house Democrats and Republicans have eighty, while Senate Democrats have sixty and Senate Republicans slightly fewer on the payroll (Rosenthal 1988).

Wherever partisan staffs are of substantial size, their overriding objective is partisan rather than legislative (Starkey 1993). In New York, it has become traditional practice to carry "no shows" on the legislative payroll, with their principal efforts devoted to political campaigns. In 1986, eight Democratic candidates for the Senate were supported by workers on the Senate payroll (Oreskes 1987).

In California, the politicization of the legislative staffs has spread to the standing committees. Before the 1960s, the committee staff was strictly non-partisan. Today, there is partisan staff on all of the State Assembly and Senate committees: "The policy experts have been replaced by the political hired guns whose main job is to get their boss reelected" (Jeffe 1987, 42).

Legislative campaign committees, similar to those operated by the congressional party caucuses in the House and the Senate, have come to play a significant role in state politics. By the middle of the 1980s, legislative campaign committees had emerged in over 30 states (Shea 1995; Salmore and Salmore 1989; Jewell and Patterson 1986). Legislative campaign committees developed in some former machine states when legislators realized that they could no longer depend on local patronage-based parties to secure their reelections. Many state legislative campaign committees not only recruit candidates for open seats and to run against vulnerable incumbents, and unlike many official party organizations, actively back candidates in primaries. Wisconsin's Democratic speaker of the House has been an active seeker of candidates for the legislature—funding those candidates from the primary to the general election (Ehrenhalt 1992).

The development of the modern state legislature, which emerged from the legislative reform movement of the 1960s and 1970s, has changed the incentives for serving in legislatures. The creation of legislative staff support for legislators, the increase in legislative compensation, the distribution of resources to rank and file legislators, and the increase in power of the state legislatures have combined to make the legislature more attractive place to embark upon a political career.

As electoral imperatives become more important in state legislatures, it is inevitable that states are moving toward increased partisan staffing. The old, nonpartisan legislative model has given way to personal and partisan staffing.

THE ENTERPRISE-IN-OFFICE: CALIFORNIA STYLE

While the growth of the legislative enterprise grew at a fairly steady pace at the national level, the California experience is nothing short of dramatic. Before the 1960s, like most state legislatures in the country, California was principally a citizen legislature. It met for a few months out of the year, legislative salaries were symbolic, and the legislature had few resources. The citizen legislator of that time was not expected to make a career of lawmaking in Sacramento. For example, during the five sessions of the 1901–1910 legislatures, the Assembly averaged fifty-six freshmen per election—a turnover of seventy percent. It is important to note that this high rate of turnover was not due to defeat but to voluntary withdrawal.[2] These high voluntary turnover rates are in sharp contrast with those today. Between 1956 and 1966, the turnover rate dropped to an average of seventeen per election for the Assembly (21 percent) and seven for the Senate (18 percent). During the post-reform period

(1967 to 1998), after the legislature increased its resources, the Assembly has averaged eight new members (10 percent) and the Senate five (13 percent). The legislature was transformed with ascension of Jesse ("Big Daddy") Unruh to the California Assembly Speakership. Jesse Unruh's role in California politics will probably be best remembered for the development of a superbly staffed, full-time, and well-paid legislature.

In 1966, through Unruh's leadership, the legislature submitted constitutional amendments to the voters in Proposition 1A. Proposition 1A allowed members of the legislature to set their own compensation. Under the provisions of the proposition, legislative salaries were set at $16,000—then the highest salaries in the United States.

Almost overnight, the California legislature was transformed from a part-time governing institution to a full-time professional legislature. One indicator of this change can be seen in Table 3.4. The length of legislative sessions dramatically increased since the passage of Proposition 1A, averaging slightly over 100 days per year prior to the reforms to essentially full-time in just a few years.

Besides the increase in salaries, the Assembly created the tools needed to handle research and program development, largely through professional staffs assigned to the committees, the best in the fifty states at the time. Individual legislators were also given large budgets to hire personal staff: secretaries, administrative legislative assistants, and field representatives, all modeled after the United States Congress. In 1955, the legislature employed 100 professional aides (Figure 3.5). In 1968, after the passage of Proposition 1A, the number of staffers had grown to nearly 500 and the legislature's operating budget was $20 million. By 1998, the state legislature employed nearly 3,000 professional staff and had an operating budget of over $165 million (Block and Buck 1999; Ainsworth 1993; Lewis 1991).

In 1967, members of the State Assembly had a personal budget of $75,000 to set up their own apparatus. By 1974, this allocation had risen to $150,000, and by 1987, nearly $400,000 (Macartney 1975; Jeffe 1987). In 1998, members of the Assembly had an average of 7.3 personal aides and State Senators 14.4.[3]

Following the same developmental lines in Congress, state legislators in California have also poured staff resources into their districts. In 1998, the average member of the Assembly had 5.9 staffers in their district and members of the State Senate 8.4. Also like members of Congress, these district-based aides are often used in the incumbent's own campaign to perform an array of activities such as fund raising or direct mail efforts. However, the use of personal staff for campaign purposes often extends beyond the individual legislator's reelection effort. Staffers can also be lent to candidates running for a new office or to incumbents who face a serious challenger. Not all

Figure 3.4
Number of Session Days in the California State Legislature, 1950–1998

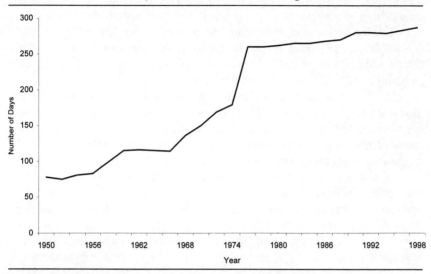

Source: Adapted from A. G. Block and Claudia Buck (1999), Stephen Green et al. (1992), and Charles G. Bell and Charles M. Price (1987, 38).

Figure 3.5
Growth of Professional Staff in the California Legislature, 1954–1998

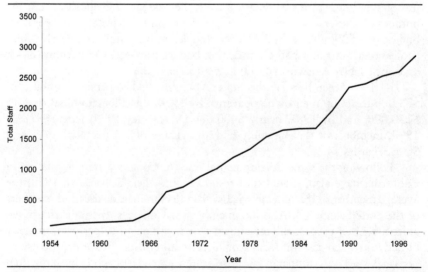

Source: Adapted from A. G. Block and Claudia Buck (1999), James Richardson (1989, 348–352), Sherry Bebitch Jeffe (1987, 42–45), and John D. Macartney (1975, 73–74).

legislators have pursued this offensive strategy, but those who chose to do so relied heavily on the expert aide. What has made the offensive strategy possible has been that campaign costs vary greatly from one election to the next. In open districts and in districts where incumbents were vulnerable, election costs rose sharply with increased competition; this meant candidates were often willing to accept aid from other legislators.

A NEW PARTY?

Los Angeles is often used as an example of a city that lacks strong parties. In the postwar years, it was an area where candidates presumably reined supreme, and the traditional party apparatus had little or no influence over their behavior. It was in this environment that James Q. Wilson (1966) traced the emergence of a new political institution, the California Democratic Council. The club movement began as an effort to fill the vacuum left by the absence of any traditional party organization. Wilson contends that, "In cities where parties are strong, that strength results from the existence of an effective precinct organization, the ability to determine who shall be the party's nominee, and control of the patronage resources of government. In California, all three sources of strength are lacking" (1962, 101). Wilson's evaluation of the traditional apparatus of the party is probably as true today as it was three decades ago. The traditional apparatus of the party certainly does not have access to significant levels of patronage (in its traditional form), the fragmentation of the various organs of the party makes coordination difficult, and until recently, it was illegal for the party to make party endorsements—a legacy of California's anti-party past.[4] But this is an evaluation of the formal party apparatus, and the new party can be found among the office holders who run a cohesive party institution.

What has emerged is an "entitlement party," a party that has automatic access to resources through its incumbents by virtue of their position in the legislature. These resources have been institutionalized in Congress and the California state legislature—incumbents now command a built-in enterprise-in-office. However, rather than viewing the incumbent's apparatus as a threat to parties, the district-based apparatus is simply the evolution of a more effective form of *party* organization. In other words, the personal political apparatus of the incumbent, working with other incumbents, performs party activities, and these include the recruitment of candidates for public office, the performance of electoral activity, and the satisfaction of the party's support base, that is, the voters.

Key to understanding the new party is the institution of political staffing. Staffers working for members of Congress, state legislators, and local public officials are the means for performing these activities and maintaining the

The Party Web

Table 3.5
Concentration of Offices in Los Angeles County

	Total Offices in L. A. County	Number of Staffers
U.S. Senate	2	33
U.S. House	22	201
State Senate	20	178
State Assembly	28	186
County Supervisor	5	182
Mayor	1	603
L.A. City Council	15	254
Total	93	1,637

Sources: These figures are derived from a number of different sources. Federal staff figures can be found in the *Congressional Staff Directory* (Washington, D.C.: Annual Edition, 1999). State figures can be found in *The California State Government Directory* (Sacramento: California Journal, 1999). Figures for city and county governments were provided by the *Los Angeles County Roster* (Los Angeles: The Los Angeles County Registrar of Voters, 1999). Excluded from the totals are volunteers working in the various field offices.

linkages between office holders. The party structure takes shape through the cooperation and collaboration of these office holder units. In Los Angeles County, the sheer concentration of offices and political aides creates the opportunity for the development of a cohesive party institution. Table 3.5 lists the number of offices in Los Angeles County with their corresponding number of political aides. In the Los Angeles County alone, there are 93 offices employing over 1,600 political aides.

The new party is increasingly recruiting from the staffs of elected officials. Just as the old party drew from the ranks of its loyal and well-trained party workers to fill open seats, the new party also draws from the ranks of its working institution, the office holder's staff. A field staffer is in a unique position to take advantage of any opening in a legislative seat. A political aide already knows what issues are important in the district and who the important groups are.

Together, the field offices promote the advancement of promising candidates for office. This promotion begins with identifying "rising stars" within the district; grooming them for office; and when a seat opens up, supporting these candidates with campaign contributions and other forms of campaign support. Nonmonetary support includes lending the candidate party workers, helping with fund-raising, and providing certain campaign services like polling. Involvement in elections flows from the presence of the political apparatus in the district. Out of this office, personnel and other resources are deployed to work on campaigns. The incumbent's personal staff is often lent to other candidates, including incumbents facing strong challengers and others running for office for the first time.

All parties must find some method for securing the resources of government to satisfy the interests of their supporters. Thus, the party must find a means to concentrate power within the formal institutions of the government. To this end, the incumbent's district office has developed into an elaborate constituency service operation. The field office helps aggrieved citizens by granting them access to governmental agencies and pushing those agencies to resolve complaints in the constituent's favor. In addition, the district apparatus, often working with other offices, can service the needs of various groups in their constituencies.

Paradoxically, growth of incumbent resources and the emergence of the new campaign technologies have coincided with greater cooperation or coordination between office holders in the party. Although both types of resources created the potential for the independence of candidates from the party, they also created new opportunities for cooperation between candidates, consultants, and the formal party apparatus. Incumbents who remain independent are taking a risk in a system where the resources of rival party incumbents, working together, can be concentrated to unseat them in the next election.

That the parties of the twentieth-century would turn to a new institution, while still maintaining the skeletal nature of their structural arrangements, should not come as a great surprise (Aldrich 1995). The debate about whether or the parties have declined may no longer be germane. This exercise implies comparison. But what are we comparing the parties with? Parties of the nineteenth-century operated in a different world than today. Even the parties of a few decades ago faced different challenges than contemporary parties. We should move beyond simplistic comparisons of contemporary parties with some stylized and nostalgic view of the way things used to be. A more useful avenue is to study parties in a contemporary environment as they attempt to meet contemporary challenges.

4

Political Staffing

Living "For" and "Off" Politics

> Those who say, 'I don't do politics,' don't belong in this
> business. I'm not making a moralistic judgment of whether
> it's right or wrong—I'm saying what is.
>
> —Congressional Aide

A BREED APART

With time demands and compensation increasing, the old breed of legislator is vanishing and a new breed is emerging in many states.[1] The old amateur legislatures, once filled with "citizen" politicians, have been transformed. In the citizen-run legislative bodies, politics was a part-time pursuit practiced by those who had careers outside the legislative institution—in business, law, and other private careers (Rosenthal 1989). This all changed when many state and local governing bodies increased legislators' salaries and their resources, especially staff, which could be used to build and maintain a personal political apparatus. The citizen politician disappeared because they could no longer compete with people who devoted all of their energies to winning and retaining public office. The decline of *practicing* attorneys is especially conspicuous. Nationally, the proportion of attorneys declined from 30 percent in 1960 to 20 percent in 1979, and was down to 16 percent in 1986 (National Conference of State Legislatures 1986).

There is a rather well-developed literature on recruitment and political ambition, and how these affect the career patterns of political leaders.[2] While studies have focused on the ambitions of many political elites, local elected officials to members of Congress, little research has addressed the recruitment and ambitions of political aides.[3]

A political life based on professionalism creates new patterns for success and advancement. It alters the potential pool of those who seek office, bringing new attitudes about public life with them. In addition, new skills and experiences are required to win public office. Legislative seats accrue to those who treat politics as a career and have the opportunity and drive to gain the skills necessary to realize the ultimate goal in politics—winning public office. As legislative staffs have become more personal and partisan, the opportunity for advancing a legislative career through staffing becomes feasible. Professional and partisan staffing is an institution that channels the politically ambitious; it supports their political activity; it provides a training and testing ground for those with ambition for political office. In short, political staffing is a recruitment apparatus for the parties. For example, in Wisconsin 17 percent of the members of the legislature served either as congressional or state legislative staffers before being elected (Backstrom 1986). Wisconsin's Speaker, the Speaker Pro Tempore, and the Democratic caucus chairman were all former legislative aides: "The staff has become a farm system for aspiring Democratic politicians" (Ehrenhalt 1992, 138). Recruited candidates are on the party mailing list, are offered campaign training, and are promised financial help. Systematic recruitment from the ranks of legislative staff is occurring only in a few states, but in many others this may be the primary path to office in the future. In California, the future is here.

THE GROWTH OF POLITICAL AIDES AS OFFICE HOLDERS

The last several decades have witnessed a dramatic increase in the number of former political aides running for and winning elected office in California.[4] This growth has been nothing short of spectacular. Figure 4.1 shows the increase in the number of former aides that comprise the California State Assembly.

In 1960, *not one* sitting member of the Assembly had experience as a political aide. Since then, the growth of former aides in the state legislature has increased at a steady pace. In 1970, 13 percent of the legislators had previous experience as staffers, and by 1980, this percentage had grown to 32 percent. By 1998, nearly 55 percent of the legislators in the State Assembly began their political careers as political aides. The number of political aides running for and winning national offices is also quite dramatic. Figure 4.2 shows the increase in the number of former aides winning congressional seats in California. As with the Assembly, in 1960, no member of Congress had previous experience as a political aide, and by 1970, this percentage had only grown to about 8 percent of the State's delegation.[5] By 1980, this percentage had more than tripled to 25 percent, and by 1998, 43 percent of California's congressional delegation had experience as a political aide. California is not the only place where former aides hold public office. In 1974 16 percent of all members of Congress had a staff background, and by 1998, this figure increased to 47 percent.[6]

Figure 4.1
Growth of Former Aides in the California Assembly, 1960–1998

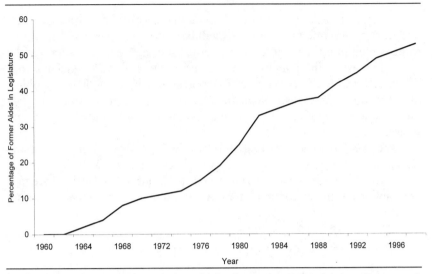

Source: Adapted from A. G. Block and Claudia Buck (1999), Stephen Green et al. (1992), John Adkisson (1979), and John D. Macartney (1975).

Figure 4.2
Growth in Former Aides in Congress (California Delegation), 1960–1998

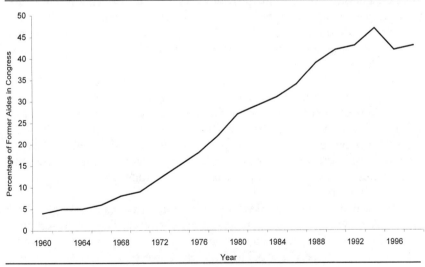

Source: Adapted from A. G. Block and Claudia Buck (1999), Stephen Green et al. (1992), John Adkisson (1979), and John D. Macartney (1975).

As state legislatures around the country become more professionalized, the former-aide-as-incumbents will be mainstays. The viability of this route is built into the institution of political staffing itself. It maximizes the opportunities for the pursuit of office and reduces the risks endemic to a life in politics. Staffing maximizes opportunities by providing the politically ambitious the skills, connections, and resources needed to be successful and it alleviates risks by permitting them to earn a living while pursuing a career in politics.

Because large-scale staffing is relatively new, the full impact of the recruitment of elected officials through political staffs is yet to be realized. Before the 1950s, there were very few staff positions, but now there are tens of thousands. If trends continue, staffing will become the primary mechanism of political candidate recruitment.

LIVING "FOR" AND "OFF" POLITICS

Max Weber wrote that "either one lives 'for' politics or one lives 'off' politics" (1958, 77–128). He went on to argue that bureaucrats could make their living off politics, but that politicians could not always count on a government salary—they require an independent source of income. However, political staffing is making it possible for people to live both for and off politics. Political staffing thus provides a significant monetary incentive for political participation *and* for a career in politics. Such a change in the incentive system could not occur without changes in the opportunities for public office. Political aides share their patron's office and exercise some of that office's influence.

A generation ago, people interested in a professional career in politics had nowhere to turn but the party. They would begin at the lower levels, working to positions of increasing responsibility and power. Eventually this faithful service would be repaid, and they would be rewarded with the party's nomination for public office. However, one by-product of the professionalization of politics is that there has been a widespread proliferation of staff positions, and as this institution has expanded, the opportunities for the politically ambitious have increased.

Political life is often unpredictable and ambition alone does not guarantee that a person will be successful in a bid for public office. Those who seek their political fortunes through volunteer party jobs must face this uncertainty. Those who begin their careers as a political staffers, however, can expect interesting and remunerative careers, even if they never attain public office.

> To tell you the truth if I wasn't receiving a paycheck I don't think
> that I would be involved in politics—at least not full-time. Politics

Table 4.1
Political Experience among Chiefs-of-Staff

	Total (50) %	Democrats (30) %	Republican (20) %	Congress (22) %	Assembly (28) %
Political Experience					
Prior Staff Experience	38	40	35	45	29
Active in Community	82	83	80	82	82
First Job in Campaign	68	70	65	73	64
Campaign Professional	46	47	45	50	43

Note: Multiple responses.
Source: Chief-of-Staff Interviews, 1992.

will always be my passion, but I also need to pay the bills. There is no other job I would rather do.
—State Legislative Aide

THE PATH TO POWER

There are nearly 1,500 political staff positions in Los Angeles County. These positions offer a new route into politics for people with talent and ambition. Staff careers permit the politically ambitious to take up politics as a vocation.

Table 4.1 displays some common elements in the political and professional experience of the chiefs-of-staff. Many chiefs-of-staff worked as staffers before accepting their current responsibilities. Thirty-eight percent have worked as full-time assistants to other incumbents. Lower level offices are stepping-stones to higher and more important staff positions. Also, because staffers often follow their patron from one seat to another as his career advances, it is not surprising that congressional aides-in-charge have more staff experience. State and local offices are more likely to be a launching point for a career in politics, both as an office holder and a political aide. Republican and Democratic political aides differ little in their staff backgrounds, suggesting that both parties may have similar recruitment patterns.

Eighty-two percent were politically active in their communities. This is an especially well-traveled recruitment path. Such activity provides useful experience, visibility, and contacts. Office holders and their aides know the activists in their district and meet with them on a routine basis. These contacts become avenues to staff recruitment.

Most have had extensive experience in politics, and began their staffing careers as a member of the incumbent's campaign team with the promise that victory would lead to a job on the incumbent's staff. Being a worker in a successful campaign is an especially viable path to a staff position since two-thirds of the chiefs-of-staff took this route. Some received their jobs because they were the office holder's campaign manager, and most still run the reelection effort. Nearly all, have done campaign work, but more importantly, 46 percent did it professionally.

Political aides carry their campaign skills and expertise into the legislative field office. This background is important because the change in job titles from a campaign manager to chief-of-staff does not mean that the nature of their duties also changes. The political skills that were useful in getting them the job with an incumbent continue to be useful in the day-to-day activities of the field office. Most of the chiefs-of-staff have held positions in the district, and do not shuttle between Sacramento and Washington and the district; they are local political specialists.

Others held positions in the legislature or in government agencies, "proving themselves in the legislative trenches."[7] One State Assembly aide started as a government bureaucrat and found herself acting as spokesperson for the agency in legislative committee hearings. She was offered a key staff position by a legislator who sat on that committee.

Another chief-of-staff had started his career by persuading his fellow workers in a small shop to organize and join the plant union. He became shop steward, and rose within the union leadership ranks for several decades. Eventually, he was engaged in a variety of electoral activities at the local, state, and federal level, "it was just part of my job."[8]

When asked about political ambitions many aides said that they would definitely follow political careers, but that they wanted no part of running for office themselves.

> I see myself as more of the behind-the-scenes kind of person. I think that is where I am most effective. If I wasn't doing this I would probably set up shop as a consultant full-time. I mean, I do it part-time now, so moving to full-time would not be that much of a stretch.
> —Congressional Aide

At least half of the top district aides can be considered careerists—they will spend their working lives as political assistants. Some see their careers revolving around a particular patron.

> I'll go where ever he goes. This position gives me the freedom to do a number of different things—I can work on campaigns; tackle certain issues; I can make a difference in certain areas of public policy. For me, there is no other job I would rather have.
> —State Legislative Aide

Many aides interviewed in Los Angeles County have political ambitions. Twenty percent say they definitely or probably will run for public office, and in some cases these plans were quite specific.

I'll start out with the [City Name] City Council. I'll probably serve there for a few terms before setting my sights on an Assembly seat. A lot of it depends on the timing. Seats can open up quite unexpectedly and you have to be ready to move when that happens. After the Assembly, I will probably run for Congress. After that, who knows?
—State Assembly Aide

Others are interested in advancing their careers even if that means switching patrons. One of the aides-in-charge lost a field representative who moved to another district in order run for a State Assembly seat. This political aide had simply been waiting for an incumbent to retire or move to a higher office. When the State Assembly incumbent announced his decision to seek a State Senate seat, this aide quit his job with his patron and moved across town.

Clearly, staffers are involved for more than a desire to influence public policy or act as a community resource. Many have a long-standing ambition for a career in politics that explains the similarity in their political experiences and skills. Additionally, the political nature of the field office make these skills useful on a day-to-day basis. A great deal has been written about the explosion of legislative staff in this country. For Congress and state legislatures, one consequence of this change has been the sheer increase in legislative activity (Fiorina 1977; Cain et al. 1987; Rosenthal 1989). However, this change has also altered recruitment patterns in this country. Political staffing provides a new route to a political career within the party, especially elective office. A more comprehensive view of political parties must focus on how staffing as an institution has evolved into a recruitment apparatus for the parties, giving those with ambitions the opportunity to be paid for their political activity. But political staffing does more than allow future office holders the financial means to "cool their heels" as they wait for an open seat. Staffing provides crucial training for those who intend to pursue public office.

5

The Enterprise-in-Office

The Legislator as a Ward Boss

> If you are going to survive and prosper—and your boss is
> going to prosper—you have to have the ability to get the
> member reelected and use the most of the power of
> incumbency. As a district staffer, if you can't work on
> campaigns, then you're disposable.
>
> —State Legislative Aide

The modern party, like the old, has developed a system that sustains a stable cadre of party workers who perform a variety of election tasks. At the core of the modern party is the incumbent's enterprise-in-office that engages in activities supportive of the parties' candidates for public office. This workforce is comprised of the locally-based field staffers who, by virtue of their position with the incumbent, are assigned a wide range of campaign chores.

THE LEGISLATOR AS AN ENTERPRISE-IN-OFFICE

As was shown in previous chapters, the growth of staffs and other resources in the late-1960s and the 1970s permits the consideration of members of Congress and state legislators as "the head of an enterprise—an organization consisting between 8 or 10 to well over 100 subordinates" (Salisbury and Shepsle 1981, 559). The usefulness of the legislator-as-organization notion arises from its capacity to encompass the individual member of Congress, state legislator, or locally elected official and his or her staff. There is no need to determine where an office holder's own activities and those of his staff begin. Rather, given the requirements of staff loyalty, legislators and their aides can be viewed as single units, however complex their operations. In the district environment, this conceptualization is even more accurate because there is no differentiation in staff loyalty to the incumbent—it is all personal, and "the core of any congressional enterprise," observe Robert Salisbury and Kenneth Shepsle, "is the *personal* staff" (1981a, 559).

The office holder's personal apparatus, as usually conceived, extends well beyond the State Capitol and Washington in three important respects. The first is that national and state elected officials' campaigns exist as ongoing operations in the district. Today, the enterprise-in-office is a full-time operation and political aides serve crucial roles in a campaign process that does not end (Kurtz 1987). Second, increasing numbers of staffers are being placed in the district to help other candidates in the area with their bids for public office (Loomis 1988).[1] Thus, the resources of the enterprise-in-office spill over into other electoral contests. Third, to sustain such operations, both state legislators and members of Congress have begun to accumulate large campaign war chests. More than fifty House members had over $275,000 on hand after the 1990 election.[2] In a related vein, growing numbers of legislators are forming their own PACs. In 1988, forty-six members of the House ran their own PACs, which contribute to their fellow members of Congress and to state and local candidates (Alston 1992; Dillin 1989; Berke 1989). However, no such mechanism is required for members of Congress to funnel their own campaign funds to other candidates, and increasing numbers are simply shifting their resources to their allies.[3] In California, state legislators have also been active in providing financial support to other candidates (Miller 1990; Edsall 1989).

Thus, the legislator is more than just an individual; the activities of his or her enterprise extend beyond the boundaries of the legislature. This chapter takes up the first of these activities, the electoral role of the field office.

THE ENTERPRISE-IN-OFFICE AND THE ENDLESS CAMPAIGN

Gary Jacobson asserts that,

> Congressional campaign organizations are personal, temporary, and, for the most part, staffed with volunteers. . . . To be sure, candidates who conduct more than one campaign—notably, incumbents—gain useful experience and develop a core of experienced campaign workers who can be called on in the future; this is another thing that strengthens their candidacies. But organizations usually still have to be put together anew each time, and each contest presents unique problems. (1987, 59–60)

This view of campaigns ignores the implications of political staff. The growth of staffers at the national, state, and local levels of government has given elected officials the resources needed to keep their campaigns up and running continuously. Staff positions are the chief way for providing material incentives for attracting campaign aides. The incumbent's staff allows him to attract and retain a stable core of workers who can be counted on to do the chores vital to the maintenance of the incumbent's personal political apparatus. This enables the incumbent to keep the nucleus of his personal apparatus intact on a permanent basis. Elections occur at regular intervals; however, the activities and the electoral advantages of the incumbent's staff are not limited by the short time before an election. The tasks performed by staffers are sustained between election cycles.

However, the literature on campaigns does not address this feature of the campaign process. The concept of the campaign as a process that occurs just before election day is a traditional view that obscures the implications of political staffing. First, it is generally assumed that campaigns are time specific events—they have a beginning, sometime before the primary, and an ending, on election day. Unless this viewpoint is reevaluated, the understanding of political staffing as an electoral resource can only be a partial one. While it is true that the incumbent's staff is visibly active during the campaign, it is far more significant that the electoral activity of the incumbent's staff is continuous. The enterprise-in-office is in constant motion, weaving together its constituency service activities with those relating to elections; it has a foot in both environments. While doing favors for individual constituents is the bread and butter of any district office, it also provides the opportunity to cultivate the support of certain groups in the district. Staffers work with these groups to mobilize volunteers, to raise campaign funds, and to turn out their supporters on election day. This process has no beginning or end; it is up and running well before the "official" campaign begins, and it continues long after it is over. Political staffing is the instrument of the endless campaign.

Another aspect of campaign studies that limit their relevance here is the almost exclusive emphasis on *strategy*, which V. O. Key defined as a general plan that "may fix the principal propaganda themes to be emphasized in the campaign, define the chief targets within the electorate, schedule the peak output of effort, and set other broad features of the campaign" (1964, 462).

The problem with this approach is that it implicitly assumes that the most important thing about a campaign is the choice of what to do. The question of resources is not addressed.[4] Although this chapter will discuss how staff resources are used to reduce electoral uncertainty for the incumbent, it is the deployment of this resource that provides clues as to the changing nature of party organization in the United States. This consistency in the performance of campaign chores is not only a benefit to the incumbent, but the involvement of political aides in campaigns outside the sphere of their boss's reelection efforts provides the party with a well-disciplined and reliable cadre of workers who work in campaigns from local city races to presidential contests.

To fully appreciate the role and value of staff as an electoral resource for the parties, an understanding of their role beyond the electoral efforts of their boss is necessary.

A BUILT-IN CAMPAIGN TEAM

The incumbent's district-based apparatus is primarily a *political* office. The staffers' involvement, especially the top aide, in electoral activity is quite extensive. In terms of direct campaign work for the incumbent, the chiefs-of-staff for members of Congress and state legislators were overwhelmingly involved in their boss's reelection efforts.[5] Staffers are involved in developing direct mail, voter registration, face-to-face canvassing, and distributing campaign literature. It is almost an unwritten law that staffers work on their boss's campaign on their own time. "If your boss doesn't win, you don't have a job—it's a matter of self-interest."[6]

Table 5.1 shows that a full 92 percent of the chiefs-of-staff reported working on their employer's campaign. Democratic political aides report slightly higher levels of involvement with their boss's reelection effort in contrast to Republican aides, while congressional and State Assembly aides report nearly identical levels of campaign involvement.

Federal and state laws permit legislative staffers to engage in this type of political activity. Similarly, political appointees in the federal executive branch are exempt from the Hatch Act, including noncareer and Schedule C appointees (e.g., White House staffers).[7] While political activity is not permitted while the employee is on government time, the distinction between legal and illegal campaign activity by field staffers is far from clear.[8] Most aides campaign while they are technically on government time. Political aides organize and attend fund-raisers, meet with various political groups, and speak at rallies. Other activities, while perhaps not considered direct campaigning for the incumbent, nonetheless have an electoral payoff. Speaking with the media, writing press releases, meeting with local groups, and mailing newsletters to constituents fall under the legitimate activities of a field office. But these activities also fall within the orbit of the campaign effort—the promotion of the incumbent's name, giving the incumbent a powerful electoral advantage over challengers. Thus, all activity blends into promotional activity, making it difficult to know where campaigning begins and ends.

All aides help on various aspects of the campaign, ranging from staffers lending a hand with a campaign project to others who oversee every aspect of the campaign. The choice is not whether to let one's aides help on the campaign, but the strategy chosen to maneuver in the gray area that separates the legitimate promotional activities of the field office from those that constitute pure campaigning. Some offices are very careful to maintain a division

Table 5.1
Chiefs-of-Staff Working on their Patron's Reelection Campaign

	Total *(50)* %	*Democrat* *(30)* %	*Republican* *(20)* %	*Congress* *(22)* %	*Assembly* *(28)* %
Worked on Patron's Reelection Campaign	92	97	85	91	93

Source: *Chief-of-Staff Interviews*, 1992.

between the legitimate office activities and those relating to the campaign. They do this in several different ways. First, some political aides take a leave-of-absence from their job to work on the campaign, thus ensuring that there is no conflict of interest. After the campaign is over, they simply are reinstated in their former position. Many aides revealed, however, that the conversion from legislative aide to campaign activist merely constituted a change in the source of their paycheck. Most continued to show up at work and do the things that they had done before they switched to the campaign. Only now they had more freedom to engage in activity that might be frowned upon as a staff employee. Others split their time between the campaign and field office, coordinating events and projects with those still working in the district office.

Staffers take leaves-of-absence not because they want to avoid a conflict of interest, but because their campaign activity constitutes a full-time job, and, as will be discussed in more detail in the next chapter, they may be doing campaign work for another candidate on behalf of their boss. Also, in several cases, the top aide in the district was employed part-time, freeing the aide to conduct political work on a full-time basis, all the while receiving two paychecks: one from the government and one from the campaign organization. This arrangement was not only convenient during the election year, but many district operations maintained this relationship throughout the incumbent's term.[9] Forty percent of the offices employed this time-splitting strategy with nearly three-quarters of the chiefs-of-staff in these offices devoting equal time to the campaign and their duties in the field office. However, most aides campaign while continuing to hold down their government jobs, working while on the job, after hours, or on the weekends. The chief-of-staff is not the only person working on the campaign, staffers throughout the incumbent's apparatus are unambiguously performing a whole array of campaign tasks. Table 5.2 shows the proportion of staffers in various governmental offices who are performing a variety campaign chores for their patron.

Table 5.2
Performance of Campaign Tasks by Field Staffers

	Total (342) %	Congress (81) %	State Senate (63) %	State Assembly (117) %	County Supervisor (15) %	City Council (66) %
Campaign Activities						
Get-out-the-Vote	48	33	49	50	53	44
Telephone Canvassing	42	35	44	45	53	46
Distribute Literature	40	35	46	43	33	33
Voter Registration	40	33	48	40	40	39
Fund-Raising	34	28	35	39	27	32
Door-to-door Canvassing	29	22	37	28	53	27

Note: Multiple responses.
Source: Marvick et al., *Field Office Study*, 1990.

Staffers are more likely to engage in activities where they make personalized contacts with voters, get-out-the-vote efforts (48 percent), telephone canvassing (42 percent), and voter registration (40 percent). Many top aides viewed this as part of the staff's role in linking the incumbent to his or her constituency, and "if we have to do this through the campaign—so be it."[10]

In terms of specific office types, a greater proportion of political aides working for state legislators and local officials performed campaign chores as opposed to their congressional counterparts. This reflects a tendency in the congressional offices to have a greater degree of specialization in the assignment of duties. For example, many congressional offices had staffers who were assigned to work exclusively on constituency casework, and it was not uncommon for them to be assigned specific types of casework, such as IRS cases. Conversely, in state and local field offices, staffers were generalists, performing many different duties, including campaign-related activity. Thus, the primary distinction between congressional and state and local offices is that congressional offices create a clearer demarcation between those political aides who are needed to work on the campaign and those who perform other activities in the field office. But as mentioned earlier, while many of these duties would not be considered pure campaigning, they nonetheless are activities supportive of the electoral effort of the district apparatus. In this support role, staffers schedule events in the district, conduct opinion polls, coordinate activities with other district organizations, and recruit and organize volunteers. In general, state and local field offices are more flexible and involve a greater proportion of the field staff in the campaign. For state offices, "the campaign is an all out effort; everyone contributes."[11]

Table 5.3
Performance of Campaign Tasks by Field Staffers by Party

	Total (342) %	Democrats (236) %	Republican (106) %
Campaign Activities			
Get-out-the-Vote	48	48	48
Telephone Canvassing	42	45	38
Distribute Literature	40	40	41
Voter Registration	40	41	38
Fund-Raising	34	33	40
Door-to-door Canvassing	29	31	25

Note: Multiple responses.
Source: Marvick et al., *Field Office Study*, 1990.

The involvement in campaign activity does not differ greatly by party (Table 5.3). Staffers working in Republican offices are just as active in the campaign as their Democratic rivals. Democrats are only slightly more likely to engage in activities such as telephone canvassing (45 percent for Democrats versus 38 percent for Republicans) and door-to-door canvassing (31 percent for Democrats versus 25 percent for Republicans), while Republican staffers are more involved in fund-raising (40 percent for Republicans versus 33 percent for Democrats), though these differences are only slight.

Republicans also have greater specialization on their staffs. Individuals who were specialists in fund-raising, media relations, or grass-roots organizing had these skills *before* becoming a member of the staff—or put another way, gained their position *because* of their skills. For example, one Republican field representative who had been involved in campaigns since she was a freshman at Indiana University developed a reputation as an effective grass-roots organizer in Indiana. She became active in California politics after graduating from college, working on several national and state campaigns. She eventually gained a position on a congressional staff and continued to organize voluntary efforts in her patron's district.

Political activity was not always considered voluntary by the district staffer. For a vast majority of these offices, the unwritten rule is that political aides are expected to work on the campaign. A congressional aide revealed:

It's a given. Let me give you an example: If I'm in a corporation and working for an entrepreneur and his business, the bottom line is that they succeed. They are hiring you to produce. Bottom line: They say 'Jump,' you say, 'How high.' If someone is coming into a

Table 5.4
Proportion of Staff Assigned to Campaign Work

	Total (50) %	Democrat (30) %	Republican (20) %	Congress (22) %	Assembly (28) %
Proportion of Staff					
0 to 25%	17	7	30	27	7
25 to 50%	13	11	15	14	11
50 to 75%	25	21	30	23	25
75 to 100%	46	61	25	36	57

Source: Chief-of-Staff Interviews, 1992.

political office, for the stuff of being social and playing with the big boys, that's not what it's all about. You have to focus on why you are there, and campaigning is the nature of the job.

A few of the chiefs-of-staff stressed that staffer involvement in the campaign was voluntary, but a majority felt that it was part of the unofficial duties of anyone working in the field office. "Besides," one congressional chief-of-staff asserted, "why else would they accept a job with a legislator if they didn't want to work on campaigns?"[12] One state legislative aide was particularly blunt about his staff's role in elections:

I find it hypocritical when staffers don't want to participate in campaigns. People outside these offices say that they are state employees, but they're not really state employees; they are hired and fired at the discretion of the member—they don't have civil service protection, and if your boss is not reelected, you don't have a job. It's pure and simple.

The question then becomes how much of the staff should be shifted to work on the campaign. Table 5.4 shows the proportion of the district staff that was assigned to do campaign work.

Nearly one-half (46 percent) of the offices assigned three-quarters or more of the staff to do some type of campaign work. The differences by party are striking. Sixty-one percent of the Democratic offices had three-quarters of their staff or more working on the campaign, while only 25 percent of Republican offices reported the same level of commitment to the campaign. This again supports the greater specialization in the Republican field offices. For Republicans, a common pattern was to employ a few staffers whose primary duties were in the campaign. In contrast, Democratic offices were more flexible, assigning workers (usually as many as possible) to the campaign as the need arose: "Today, I'm a caseworker, but if you come back next week you'll see me going door-to-door for the campaign."[13]

State Assembly offices are also more likely to shift a greater proportion of their staff resources to work on campaigns. Fifty-seven percent of the state field offices assigned three-quarters or more of the staff to do campaign work, while only 36 percent of congressional offices match this level of staff deployment. This perhaps reflects the greater number of staffers in congressional offices, reducing the need to deploy a majority of one's staff to work on the campaign.

Clearly, the level of involvement in the elections is pervasive across office level and party. For some activities, such as get-out-the-vote efforts, nearly one-half of all staffers in the Los Angeles area participated. This constitutes a rather sizable group of campaign workers. In all, elected officials in Los Angeles County operate 93 local offices, employing nearly total 1,500 professional political aides.[14] The sheer number of political aides and their level of involvement in elections insures that they have an enormous impact of the way elections are conducted in the area.

This level of involvement by staffers in elections gives the incumbent a built-in nucleus of highly effective campaign workers. They have the advantage of knowing the territory: they know what issues are important in the district; they know what volunteers can be tapped for large-scale events; and they have a familiarity with the dynamics of the area that is unmatched by "outsiders." The incumbent can field a publicly-financed team of campaign workers to do jobs for which they are well-trained—activities that are performed on a continuous basis.

RUNNING THE CAMPAIGN

Besides simply helping out on various campaign-related activities, many political aides were in charge of various campaign events. Table 5.5 shows the proportion of staffers who reported that they were directly responsible for various facets of the campaign.

As was seen in Table 5.2, fewer congressional staffers engage in campaign activity when compared to state and local aides; however, Table 5.5 shows that they are more likely to have direct responsibility for running various campaign projects. This is especially true for activities like fund-raising, with 16 percent of congressional staffers reporting that they were responsible for fund-raising efforts as compared to only 5 percent and 9 percent of State Senate and State Assembly political aides, respectively.

This perhaps suggests that the congressional staffers perform more specialized tasks. Staffers for city council members are more likely than any group to be in charge of various facets of the campaign. The irony here is

Table 5.5
Proportion of Staffers Who Were Responsible for
Running Campaign Activity by Office Type[a]

	Total (342) %	Congress (81) %	State Senate (63) %	State Assembly (117) %	County Supervisor (15) %	City Council (66) %
Campaign Activities						
Get-out-the-Vote	14	11	8	5	13	14
Telephone Canvassing	12	15	11	9	20	9
Distribute Literature	11	15	11	15	7	18
Voter Registration	8	12	10	7	7	12
Fund-Raising	13	16	5	9	7	21
Door-to-door Canvassing	10	15	10	7	7	18

[a] Those indicating that they were responsible for the operation of the specific campaign activity or project.
Note: Multiple responses.
Source: Marvick et al., *Field Office Study*, 1990.

that offices at this level are nonpartisan, a legacy of California's progressive and anti-party past, yet staffers at this level are a highly political group. In Table 5.6, the proportion of those responsible for various campaign tasks is broken down by party. Again, there is little difference between the staffers in terms of party affiliation.

Burdett Loomis found that, among aides working for new members of Congress, the most common background for congressional Administrative Assistants was experience as a campaign manager (1979, 53). These findings were confirmed in my interviews with the chiefs-of-staff with the added significance that, just because the top aide now has a job with the incumbent, this does not mean that he or she is no longer a campaign manager.

Nearly one-third of the chiefs-of-staff were in charge of their boss's last campaign. "That's what I was hired to do—to run the campaign, and we never stop campaigning."[15] Table 5.7 details the various types of people the incumbent used to run his last campaign. The chiefs-of-staff were asked who ran the last campaign: a paid campaign manager or campaign firm, an aide in the office, or the incumbent himself.

According to Table 5.7, 54 percent of the incumbents used an outside campaign manager or firm to run the campaign; however, 33 percent used their top aide in the district to run his reelection effort. For political aides running the incumbent's election bid, the amount of time spent campaigning varied considerably. Incumbents facing formidable challengers often had a

Table 5.6
Proportion of Staffers Who Were Responsible for
Running Campaign Activity by Party

	Total (342) %	Democrats (236) %	Republican (106) %
Campaign Activities			
Get-out-the-Vote	14	15	13
Telephone Canvassing	12	14	8
Distribute Literature	11	11	11
Voter Registration	8	8	8
Fund-Raising	13	12	14
Door-to-door Canvassing	10	11	8

Note: Multiple responses.
Source: Marvick et al., *Field Office Study*, 1990.

Table 5.7
Those Running the Last Campaign

	Total (50) %	Democrat (30) %	Republican (20) %	Congress (22) %	Assembly (28) %
Ran the Reelection Campaign					
Paid Manager / Firm	54	50	60	64	46
Staffer in Office	33	36	29	26	42
Incumbent	12	14	10	12	12

Note: The last campaign was the incumbent's last reelection bid, and in the case of freshmen legislator, it was their first campaign for that seat.
Source: *Chief-of-Staff Interviews*, 1992.

staffer take a leave-of-absence from their government job to run the campaign for the entire election year. Others, facing less competitive races, managed to run the campaign after hours or on the weekends. This blending of roles was made easier because many incumbents maintain a full-time campaign office next door to his district office. In at least two cases, the chief-of-staff was married to the incumbent's campaign manager.

For many chiefs-of-staff, the line between being the incumbent's top aide in the district and the campaign manager was quite thin. One of these aides asserted that, "In a campaign structure, there is no such thing as a, quote, campaign manager. You have a consultant who usually works some place far away from the district and who writes the [direct] mail. And then you have an on-site campaign person—the best on-site campaign person is the person who actually works in that neighborhood, the person running the district office."[16]

Many staffers described this as one way that the "new" and the "old" politics are merged in the campaign. The coordination of electoral activity in the district office resembles the old-fashioned techniques of reaching voters. The chief-of-staff organizes door-to-door efforts in the district, meets with the district's various groups, and coordinates different events in the district. These techniques are merged with those of the campaign specialist, such as direct mail, polling, and fund-raising.

Turning again to Table 5.7, 14 percent of Democratic aides revealed that the incumbent himself ran the campaign, while slightly fewer Republican aides (10 percent) reported that the incumbents ran their own reelection efforts. In most of these cases, the top aide was actually handling the day-to-day business associated with the campaign. In part, this was a disagreement about what was meant by "running the campaign." These were top aides who, even while handling all of the particulars of the reelection campaign, nonetheless said that their boss "ran" the campaign because he made the final decision about what was to be done or how much was to be spent.

THE POLITICAL STAFFER AS A CAMPAIGN SPECIALIST

The field office monitors events and people throughout the constituency in a comprehensive, subtle, and continuous way. At the head of this intelligence gathering operation is the chief aide. The control of information makes most top aides local political specialists.

The chiefs-of-staff were asked what kind of involvement they had in developing the content of advertising or newsletters, in developing issues or planning what questions to ask in an opinion survey. All of them acknowledged being consulted since they were the primary source of information concerning the district and its constituency. Designing polls or creating a campaign advertisement requires an intimate knowledge of the issues and groups in their constituency—and they were the resident experts.

Political aides also perform highly specialized tasks in the campaign. For many aides, their skill as campaigners was not only why they were hired by the campaign organization, but is also the reason they retain their position as a staffer with the incumbent. The staffer-as-campaign specialist has been around for a decade or more. For example, Tim Wirth's 1982 campaign for Congress used staffers to run the entire campaign—media buying, commercials, fund-raising, and direct mail (Bonafede 1982, 1599). The technical nature of modern campaigns requires more than armies of foot soldiers to get the vote out. Today, incumbents surround themselves with pollsters, fund-raisers, direct mail specialists, and media experts. However, many of these specialists can be found on the incumbent's staff. According to one veteran of many campaigns in Los Angeles:

> My firm is in the business of providing the whole array of campaign services, but often members of the incumbent's staff take over certain functions, and though I'm reluctant to admit it, they do a better job in some areas than we could ever do. Take, for example, fund raising events. At the very least you need to work with the staff in order to draw up the contribution lists. They are the ones who over the years have established and maintained the contacts with the people and organizations that will give money. So while we handle as many pieces of the campaign as possible, the candidate's staff handles often as much or more than we do.
> —Campaign Consultant

Elections are still a cyclical business and working for an incumbent allows one to earn a steady paycheck. Most district offices have a political person who, while on the job, performs some specialized campaign work, such as fund-raising, organization of volunteers, public relations, or direct mail.[17] Our conventional wisdom suggests that incumbents are captives of the consulting profession. However, what the results here suggest is that many office holders have to go no further than their staffs to receive the technical skills required to mount a sophisticated campaign. The range of campaign skills that political aides offer incumbents was extremely diverse.[18]

> I think I get more job security out of it. I'm doing a lot of extra work and saving [my boss] a lot of money. What that means is that if he doesn't have to spend it on an expensive political consultant—that he can have a staff member put it [direct mail] together to send out to the people—he can do a lot more things in the district.
> —State Legislative Aide

An indication of the highly technical role that staffers play is revealed in Table 5.8. The staffers were asked about their involvement in certain key aspects of the campaign process, including the planning of opinion surveys, the development of issues for the campaign, designing the content of direct mail and political advertising, and the coordination of various aspects of the campaign such as resolving conflicts in the organization, running the campaign headquarters, or candidate selection for other races.

Table 5.8 displays the remarkable level of staff involvement in key aspects of the campaign. Forty percent of the staffers assist in the development of

Table 5.8
Proportion of Staffers Performing Specialized Campaign Activity[a]

	Total (342) %	Congress (81) %	State Senate (63) %	State Assembly (117) %	County Supervisor (15) %	City Council (66) %
Campaign Role						
Issue Development	40	35	43	42	38	50
Campaign Coordination	38	41	34	39	32	54
Direct Mail	33	32	27	40	30	33
Campaign Conflicts	31	26	37	35	25	36
Running Headquarters	29	30	26	23	23	36
Planning Surveys	27	23	18	31	24	42
Advertising	18	20	15	19	9	38
Candidate Selection	15	21	26	12	10	27

[a] Those indicating "some involvement" to "key advisor."
Note: Multiple responses.
Source: Marvick et al., *Field Office Study*, 1990.

issues for the campaign. This level of involvement in issue development is not surprising considering that a major aspect of their job, and a principle function of the field office, is to be a political listening post, the eyes and ears of their members in the district. Knowing what issues are important is what they do best. A district apparatus has two primary functions. The first is the collection of information: what are your opponents doing, what are your critics saying?

In modern campaigns, vast resources are expended to gather and process information. For incumbents, the information gathering process is always in place—they already know what issues are important to their constituents through the monitoring of constituent mail, fielding of questionnaires in the district, and the deployment of field representatives who maintain regular contact with the active groups in the district.

The other function is the dissemination of information. The district office is responsible for letting its constituents know what the incumbent is doing, especially what he is doing for them. Sending out newsletters, speaking with the local press, and inviting constituents to "open houses" in the field office serve to keep constituents abreast of the member's activities. Another important aspect of communicating with one's constituency entails using the community as a resource to lobby for important legislation, influence the policies of various governmental agencies, or support a local candidate for office.[19] Well-maintained channels of communication with influential groups can be used to mobilize support to accomplish the incumbent's objectives, in and out of the legislature.

The chiefs-of-staff also work closely with the consultants hired to help in various aspects of the campaign. The staffers' central role in the gathering of information makes them an invaluable resource for anyone hired to do direct mail or other forms of political advertising. Turning again to Table 5.8, 33 percent of all the staffers reported being involved with the campaign's direct mail effort, 27 percent with the development of opinion surveys, and 18 percent with its advertising effort. Political aides also are used as logistical support for the campaign. Thirty-eight percent of the field staffers coordinated various aspects of the campaign, 31 percent resolved conflicts that arose in the campaign, and 29 percent offered some aid in running the campaign's headquarters. One campaign consultant revealed:

> My favorite saying is that all you need to run a campaign in Los Angeles is three people: one person to do the polling, one person to raise the funds, one person to coordinate the day-to-day activities of the campaign—all linked together with fax machines. But I know that it takes more than that. There are a multitude of little details that have to be taken care of. And without a staff that willing to work on campaigns, these things are just difficult to do.

Fifteen percent of staffers were consulted on the selection of candidates for other offices in the area. This is an indication of the central role that staffers play in the electoral process. This figure for candidate selection is even higher for political aides in congressional offices (21 percent), State Senate offices (26 percent), and for those working for members of the Los Angeles City Council (27 percent).

Some consultants work for a group of incumbents who have a long history of working together in campaigns. This draws into their orbit several different staffs working for incumbents at different levels of government.[20] For this reason, incumbents in Los Angeles County rarely campaign in isolation. Political aides are coordinating their activity with other staffs in the area and with the consultants working for these candidates. This aspect of the campaign will be dealt with in greater detail in the next chapter.

THE BLURRING OF ROLES: CONSTITUENCY SERVICE AND CAMPAIGNING

The "endless campaign" blends the constituency service activities of the field office with those in the campaign. The argument here is that the constituency service performed by the field office and their role in the campaign are interdependent. Most, if not all, of the campaign tasks performed by staffers are specific to the district office environment. In this instance, these are skills that staffers gain from performing their everyday jobs. At base, all staffers perform information-gathering tasks: what issues are important to the constituents; what problems exist in the community; who are the important groups; which community leaders are important and which ones can be ignored; who votes and who doesn't? This is information that most staffers are well-acquainted with, long before the official campaign begins. All this is done as part of the process of representing not only the district's interests in the legislature, but also the incumbent's interests among his constituents.

> Constituency service and campaigning really go hand in hand. It's really hard to know where one begins and the other ends. If you're out there representing the member in the district, informing the constituents about the issues that are affecting them, you're not only doing a good job at representation, but this also means you're laying the groundwork for the campaign. It's a two-way street. When we meet with the groups in our district, we're trying to find out what their concerns are, but we're also seeking their support. They, in a sense, become part of the team.
> —Congressional Aide

Working with certain groups in the community on issues that are important to them translates into influence on election day. This type of pull among certain constituent groups is not always confined to the district's boundaries. Staffers experienced working with certain ethnic groups have contact with its leaders all over the state, and in some cases, all over the country. In fact, incumbents often use the appointment of members of certain groups to the staff to cultivate their support. In some cases, groups within the incumbent's constituency are allowed to select their own representative on the staff. Political aides may represent labor, homosexual, or environmental organizations. Far more common, however, is the appointment of members of various ethnic groups that populate Los Angeles County. African-American, Latino, or Asian members of the staff are not only used for communicating with these groups, but also for enlisting their support during the election.[21] Both Democrats and Republicans cultivate groups in this way. For example, a Republican congressional chief-of-staff reported that, because of the enormous rise in the number of Vietnamese constituents in his district, it was important that they hire a Vietnamese staffer who could maintain contact with this new group in their district—knowing how to read and speak Vietnamese was necessary, since many local newspapers were printed in Vietnamese.[22] In a Democratic State Assembly office, the chief-of-staff required that all of her staffers speak Spanish, and those that did not before they began their job, promptly signed up for lessons.[23]

The goal of this chapter was to show the extent to which political aides, and by extension the enterprise-in-office, are involved in electoral politics. Being involved in elections did not differ greatly by office type nor party. Even at the nonpartisan local level, political aides are extremely active in the campaign. The enterprise-in-office wages an "endless campaign" weaving together its public service role as a provider of assistance to citizens and its role as a resource for elections. The result is a combination of processes that are unique to these field operations.

The district office acts as a vehicle for a range of political activity. All of the chiefs-of-staff asserted that they must take a role in it. The chiefs-of-staff become campaign specialists by virtue of their political experience.

However, this is but the first step. Involvement in campaigns does not, alone, demonstrate that there has been a change in the nature of party organization in the United States. It is a necessary, but not sufficient, condition. What is missing is an account of how these resources are used to sustain some notion of the party's institution. This is the task of the next chapter.

6

The Party Network

Electoral Cooperation and Lending

It's a political office—I've taken time off to run campaigns.
Mostly we get involved in local campaigns. When my boss
endorses someone, that means I'm going to take some time
off to run campaigns.
                                        —Congressional Aide

This chapter attempts to weave the campaign activities of the district
apparatus into a larger system of offices that work together to influence
electoral outcomes. Clearly, political staff labor for their patrons to see that
they win elections, but they also help other candidates in their bids for public
office.

What has emerged in California in not just the transfer of campaign
funds from one candidate to another, but more wide-ranging electoral intervention. An important element of this new system is the staffer as cam-
paigner. Not only do staffers take leaves to run their employer's campaign,
they are also lent to other candidates, especially those running for offices
within the legislator's own district. Members of Congress and state legislators
have been entangled in this network, and electoral intervention even extends
into local elections. The lending of staff could take the form of the aide simply
working in his spare time for another candidate, or it could entail being taken
off the legislator's payroll so that he could work on the campaign full-time. The
lending of expertise, whether for general campaign management or for more
specialized tasks, such as fund raising, has created networks of obligation
between public officials that stand parallel to the traditional party apparatus.

In the last twenty years, there has been an important change in the role
of elected officials in California electoral politics. What was formerly criticized
as a system of every person for himself, with individual candidates largely
working on their own, has become a system in which powerful incumbents
intervene regularly in other election contests.

POLITICAL STAFF: THE PARTY CADRE

If it is to perform campaign tasks a party must recruit participants to carry them out. The number of activists a party requires depends on several factors, including the number of voters in its territory, the techniques available for stimulating voter support, the costs of these techniques, and the political geography of the territory. Although opinion polling, direct mailings to voters, and television advertising have reduced the size of the workforce required for certain kinds of campaign activity, a core of stable workers is still a necessity in any successful campaign. In the nineteenth century, this consideration was key to the growth of party institutions based on a small group of party leaders. The parties had access to patronage-supported jobs for the performance of election tasks, and this was the basis of the leadership's influence over electoral outcomes.

From the middle of the twentieth century, the parties' *formal* role as the sole supplier of campaign services has declined. For many, the loss of patronage by the parties is the single most important reason that they are unable to perform the electoral functions that were performed in the past. Two decades ago, Robert Agranoff (1972) argued that the new style in politics was characterized by individual candidates and their personal organizations, rather than the parties. Since then, research has increasingly focused on the individual candidate as an important element, if not the most important element, in the electoral process (Mayhew 1986; Fiorina 1977; Schlesinger 1985; Goldberg and Traugott 1984; Wattenberg 1984).

Richard Fenno speculated that the presence of large congressional staffs in some states was an indication of the lack of traditional party organizations in these areas. Noting the large number of district staffers in California, he wrote:

> The suggestion is, then, that in states with weak party organizations (e.g., California) district staffs may be large because they are surrogate electoral organizations. (1978, 45–47)

Fenno also speculated that greater levels of electoral activity are associated with larger district operations. While unable to confirm Fenno's hunch about the relationship between staff size and electoral activity, I will explore the idea that field offices have not only become surrogate electoral organizations, but really represent a classic party organization. However, this depends on some form of collaboration or cooperation in the electoral phase. Lacking this, the enterprise-in-office is nothing more than an institutionalized campaign apparatus with the *sole* aim of reelecting the incumbent. But the evidence in this chapter suggests that the enterprise-in-office is lodged in a network of offices coordinating their electoral efforts.

Table 6.1
Coordination of Election Plans by Office

	Total (50) %	Congress (22) %	State Assembly (28) %
All Offices (at least one office)	46	41	50
County Supervisor	16	14	18
Congress	18	18	18
State Senate	24	27	21
State Assembly	24	27	21
City Council	20	23	18
School Board	12	9	14
United States Senator	16	23	11
Governor	14	14	18

Note: Multiple responses.
Source: Chief-of-Staff Interviews, 1992.

ELECTORAL COOPERATION BETWEEN FIELD OFFICES

Table 6.1 shows the level of electoral coordination between the various district offices in Los Angeles County.[1]

These are offices that coordinated some aspect of their campaign with another political office. Forty-six percent of the offices coordinated elections plans with at least one other field office. One picture that emerges from Table 6.1 is that the electoral coordination between field offices is not confined to an office's particular sphere of governmental responsibility. That is, congressional offices are coordinating with state level offices that are, in turn, coordinating their campaign plans with local offices. In 1988, for example, several members of Congress, including congressmen Henry Waxman, Howard Berman, and Mel Levine, sent mailers to their constituents promoting the state and local candidates running in their districts. In addition, this group often coordinates fund-raisers and financial contributions to other candidates in Los Angeles (Miller 1990).

This cross-jurisdictional coordination of electoral efforts is fostered by a network of former aides who move on to work for other elected officials in the area. The coordination of activity is made easier because staffers in another district office are often former assistants to the chief-of-staff.[2] A chief-of-staff for a long-time member of Congress reported that he could call on aid from at least twelve other offices because many of his aides received jobs with other elected officials in the area:

> I have my staffers, he asserted, all over the place. If there is a particularly important campaign coming up, it's important to pull all of these resources together. For every aide I have somewhere else, I can usually count on getting something from their office.

Coordinating aspects of the campaign can be a way of cutting costs or eliminating the reproduction of effort, such as fielding the same poll or sending multiple mailers. However, cooperation in the campaign goes well beyond a desire to cut costs or improve efficiency. An incumbent's willingness to coordinate all or part of the campaign with another candidate also stems from the desire to influence the outcome of elections that may have an impact on his constituency. Local races are often targets of this kind of activity from congressional and state offices, and the opportunities for this type of paternalism are quite significant. Many incumbents have two or three incorporated cities within their districts' boundaries. Only 10 percent of the chiefs-of-staff reported that their boss had a standing policy for staying out of local contests, and 12 percent of those interviewed offered some kind of campaign assistance to candidates at the local level. Some offices go as far as running a group of candidates for local city races as a team, sharing volunteers, polls, and direct mail.[3] In one such case, a member of the Assembly sponsored three candidates for seats on the city council in his district. The candidates used the same workers, raised money at the same fund-raisers, sent out a single mailer with all of them prominently displayed on the cover. And on election day, they were all victorious.

Field offices that coordinated their election plans with another office also report greater levels of campaign activity than offices that campaign in isolation. In Table 6.2, various campaign activities are compared to whether an office coordinated its election plans with another political office.[4] Although levels of activity are high for both kinds of offices, those that coordinate their election plans with other offices are more likely to engage in campaign activity.

The previous set of tables displays two important features of this system. The first is that a significant proportion of elected officials are coordinating their election plans with other offices in the area. Nearly one-half (46 percent) of the offices reported collaborating during the campaign with at least one other office. In addition, higher levels of campaign activity by the field office go hand-in-hand with the coordination of electoral plans during the campaign. The second, and perhaps the most important feature, is that this activity extends across different sectors of governmental responsibility. Congressional offices are cooperating with those at the state and local level, and state level

Table 6.2
Performance of Campaign Tasks and Electoral Cooperation

	Noncooperative Offices (27) %	Cooperative Offices (23) %
Campaign Activities		
Get-out-the-Vote	41	70
Telephone Canvassing	41	65
Voter Registration	37	61
Distribute Literature	29	57
Fund-Raising	26	52
Door-to-door Canvassing	25	43

Note: Multiple responses.
Source: Chief-of-Staff Interviews, 1992.

offices with those above and below them. This mirrors one of the celebrated by-products of the urban machines—they were able to consolidate political efforts in elections that were otherwise fragmented by multiple layers of government. The system was undoubtedly more centralized under the urban machines; however, the present system is a far cry from the chaos that characterizes many descriptions of contemporary party politics.

LENDING STAFF:
LINKAGES IN THE PARTY'S STRUCTURE

For many, the fact that political aides engage in campaign activity simply confirms a trend that has been occurring in American politics for the last several decades: the further entrenchment of incumbents in "safe" districts (e.g., Mayhew 1974). According to this view, incumbents are using the tools of incumbency to make themselves impervious to political challenge, and this includes using staffers on the public payroll to play a role in the campaign. Morris Fiorina similarly argues that "congressmen have altered their institutional surroundings in order to facilitate the performance of electorally profitable activities," and that "Presumably the district offices are totally absorbed in constituency service" (1977, 56, 59).

The above characterization is accurate in one sense: at all levels of government, elected officials have acquired resources to establish and maintain personal, political apparatuses, which are geared toward insuring their electoral success. However, the political activity of the field staff is not confined to working on their patron's campaign. Indeed, the fact that some incumbents face little serious political challenge gives them the opportunity to use their electoral resources to deploy in other campaigns. As an electoral resource, staffers serve a dual and, at times, conflicting role in the electoral process. On the one hand, they are used to make incumbents feel more secure. Having a full-time nucleus of campaign workers deployed in the district, waging an endless campaign, is a powerful electoral tool. On the other hand, when elected officials combine these resources to contest elections, which have nothing to do with their own reelection efforts, staffers then become powerful weapons to use *against* incumbents in the opposing party. So, rather than being consumed by casework, staffers are busy working on campaigns within a network of incumbents who pool their efforts to influence electoral outcomes. Fiorina's argument that staffers are an *electoral resource* still applies; however, their impact moves far beyond an indirect electoral payoff through the disbursement of mini-favors to constituents. The political aides' influence is felt as a direct participant in the campaign process, often for candidates other than their boss.

A major resource in campaigns is still people, and one of the most prevalent forms of incumbent intervention in elections is through the shifting of personnel to help in other campaigns. In many cases, this is to aid a challenger attempting to knock off a vulnerable incumbent. Often, staffers are shifted to protect an incumbent who may be facing a serious challenger; resources are sent to marginal districts where someone is in trouble or when a seat becomes competitive.[5]

Table 6.3 shows the frequency of lending staff by incumbents. In 1988 primary and general election cycles, only 26 percent of the incumbents reported *not* lending staff, while nearly one-half (48 percent) reported lending staff to three or more campaigns.[6] The difference between Democrats and Republicans is interesting. Eighty percent of the Democratic incumbents lent their staff to help in at least one campaign, while only 65 percent of the Republican incumbents did the same.

The difference between incumbents at the national and state levels of government is also significant. Eighty-two percent of the congressional offices reported lending staff as compared to only 69 percent of the state offices. This difference can be explained by the recent staff cutbacks in the state legislative offices with the passage of the state Proposition 140, which called for a 40 percent rollback in the State's legislative operating budget. Many state legislative aides reported that, since the cutbacks, it became more difficult to find people to work on campaigns.[7]

Table 6.4 displays the specific office level where staffers were sent to aid in another candidate's campaign. Given their greater resources, it is not surprising that congressional offices report higher levels of lending at every level of government as compared to their state legislative counterparts.

Table 6.3
Frequency of Lending Staff to Other Campaigns

	Total (50) %	Democrat (30) %	Republican (20) %	Congress (22) %	Assembly (28) %
Number of Campaigns					
None	26	20	35	18	31
1 to 2	26	23	30	27	27
3 or more	48	57	35	55	42

Source: Chief-of-Staff Interviews, 1992.

Table 6.4
Lending Staff to Other Campaigns and Office Level

	Total (50) %	Democrat (30) %	Republican (20) %	Congress (22) %	Assembly (28) %
Office Level					
National	25	21	30	32	19
State	65	79	45	73	58
Local	42	39	45	50	35

Note: Multiple responses.
Source: Chief-of-Staff Interviews, 1992.

According to Table 6.4, Democrats are more active staff lenders at the state level, while Republicans are more active at the local and national levels. The higher incidence of state level lending between Democrats coincides with a series of very competitive state races in the last election. In these races, staff lending occurred even before the general election began.

In 1990, Several Assembly seats were targeted by a group of office holders who regularly work together in elections, and campaign assistance was promised to these candidates *prior* to the primaries. In one of these Assembly races, the entire Democratic candidate's campaign team was staffed by political aides working for this group of office holders—the candidate's campaign manager was a congressional aide, his fund-raising was coordinated by two state legislative aides, and his mailers were handled by another state legislative aide allied with this group.[8] This member of the Assembly first won the seat in 1988 with the aid of this group, and barely retained it in 1990. Besides these key members of his campaign team, staffers from all over the Los Angeles

County worked on the campaign, running registration drives, distributing campaign literature, and going door-to-door contacting voters. Concerning this hard-fought race for the State Assembly seat, a Democratic congressional aide reported:

> The [member of the Assembly's] race? Yea, we all worked on that one. He really called in his IOUs to get people to work during the election. He used to be a staffer himself, so he knew how the system worked and he had the connections with the other elected officials in the area. There were staffers from all over L.A. County working on that one.

Lending staff is one way that elected officials can build up an informal network of obligation. Incumbents can use the electoral resources at their disposal as a way of insuring that they will have support if they ever have to face a serious challenger.[9] A congressional aide described her role in a Los Angeles City Council race in this way:

> I worked on her campaign because I moved into her district—and frankly, who knows, I may need a favor from her some day.

Another reason for lending your staff out involves the ties of friendship that exist between two incumbents. After long years of serving in the same legislative body, fellow incumbents can often count on their colleagues to lend them a helping hand in a particularly tough race.[10]

The lending of staff occurs on a fairly large scale as well. Many political aides either worked on, or were the recipients of, a large organized effort to turn out as many paid staffers as possible. In these cases, several office holders will solicit help from all over the County, or even from the State Capital. A State Assembly race, which was the site of a special election after the seat was vacated by the incumbent, drew staffers from congressional, State Senate, and State Assembly field offices all over Los Angeles County. It gave the candidate a ready-made campaign work force:

> They will call us and say, 'What can we do?' Sometimes we say, 'We need a lot of people on Saturday, can you send any of your staff over?' You can get hundreds of people that way.
> —State Legislative Aide

In this race, the Assembly candidate's congressional allies sent around a memo requesting aid from all over the county.[11] Being part of a network of incumbents gives a candidate a large pool of workers that can be tapped to work on the campaign.[12]

THE ALLOCATION OF STAFF AID

There are several conditions that may account for why staffers are lent to other candidates. An incumbent may want to extend his influence among his colleagues, to repay a debt of campaign help in the past, or the recipient of the aid may be a protégé or ally. Electoral pressures may be another condition that coincides with staff lending. Competitive races appear to attract more aides than others. At least in the Democratic party in Los Angeles, office holder cooperation in elections also appears to have a strong ethnic component. African-American, Latino, and Jewish office holders work closely together in their districts and elections.

To test some of these ideas, a probit model was used to determine which factors explain staff allocation patterns in elections. The office holders were divided into two groups: those who received aid in the last election and those who did not. Staff lending was counted as the political staff of one office holder working on the election of another. This work could entail the deployment of staffers to work on get-out-the-vote efforts in the district, helping with a fund-raiser, or an aide handling a candidate's press relations.

As independent variables, the model included whether the recipient of the aid was a former staffer, the recipient's past lending behavior, the competitiveness of the district, the donor's and recipient's ethnicity, the office type, and party.

The candidate's staffing background was included because, as a former staffer, an individual may have been active in elections in the past and could use these connections to call for help in the future. The recipient's past lending behavior tested whether allocation patterns followed the familiar pattern of *quid pro quo*, that is, one could expect aid only if they had given it in the past. The competitiveness of the district was included to determine if electoral pressures spurred staff lending. The ethnicity factor was tested by counting an ethnic "match" if the donor and recipient of the aid were of the same ethnic background.[13] For example, a Latino office holder who lent staff to another Latino candidate for office was counted as a "match." Also included as variables were party and the office type, congressional or State Assembly.

The results are presented in Table 6.5. Equation 1 includes all of the variables except the district's competitiveness. The initial results support the argument that the ethnicity of the donor and the recipient affects how decisions are made about whom should receive staff assistance. However, unrelated to lending is the recipient's past lending behavior, party, the office type, and whether the recipient was a former staffer. This suggests that allocation patterns are not necessarily dependent on rules based on reciprocal lending or the staffer's previous employment as a political aide. In addition, staff allocation patterns did not differ by office level or party, thus lending behavior

Table 6.5
Factors Affecting the Allocation of Staff Aid

Dependent Variable: Received Staffer Aid	Equation 1	Equation 2
Independent Variables		
Candidate Was Former Staffer	.58	1.43
	(.48)	(.80)
Candidate Lent Staffers in the Past	−.38	−.38
	(.52)	(.72)
Office Type (Federal or State)	−.71	−.91
	(.47)	(.78)
"Match" of Recipient's and Donor's Ethnicity	2.46***	1.68
	(.68)	(.97)
Competitiveness of the District	—	.24**
		(.01)
Party	.08	.18
	(.49)	(.64)
Constant	−.50	3.26*
	(−.75)	(1.61)
−2 Log Likelihood		
At Convergence	−22.10	−12.68
Initial	−34.66	−34.66
Percent Correctly Predicted	80	88

Asymptotic errors are reported in the parentheses. Observations: 50. * $p < .05$, ** $p < .01$, *** $p < .001$. The dependent variable is a dichotomous variable: 0 (received no aid) and 1 (received aid). An office was recorded as receiving staff aid if staffers from one office holder worked on the campaign of another. No distinction was made between office level. An office was counted as receiving aid from another officeholder of the same ethnicity regardless of office type or the proximity of the district. The district's competitiveness was measured by taking the election returns for the 1988 general election. The figures were subtracted from 50 percent to derive a competitiveness scale. The scale was reversed so that it ran from least to most competitive races.

is similar for federal and state level incumbents as well as Democratic and Republican offices.

When the district's competitiveness is added to the model in equation 2, the ethnicity factor no longer retains its explanatory power. Competitiveness, it appears, exerts a greater influence over allocation patterns. Thus, resources flow into those districts where help is needed, regardless of the recipient's and the donor's ethnicity.

The results of equation 2 correspond to the accounts of staff lending described by the chiefs-of-staff. According to the chiefs-of-staff, highly com-

Table 6.6
The Effects of Lending on the District Offices' Political Involvement

	Total (50) %	Nonlending Offices (13) %	Lending Offices (37) %
Political Involvement			
Encourage a Run for Office	67	42	75
Member of Staff Left to Consult	65	33	75
Chief Plans to Run	38	—	50
Staffer Ran for Office	19	8	24

Note: Multiple responses.
Source: Chief-of-Staff Interviews, 1992.

petitive races draw staff personnel from locations throughout Los Angeles County, and this appears to drive staff allocation patterns in elections. This, of course, is the type of behavior that best represents how linkages between offices create an effective party institution. The structural properties of the institution are flexible, responding to the electoral pressures in the area. Contesting elections is at the heart of why parties exist at all, and the political apparatuses of incumbents are dominating this core function.

THE CONSEQUENCES OF LENDING

The differences between offices that lend out their staff and those that do not are striking. The field offices that lend personnel are staffed by political aides who engage in more sophisticated types of political activity. Table 6.6 compares offices that lend their staffs with those that do not. The chiefs-of staff were asked: 1) whether they had ever encouraged someone to run for political office, 2) whether a member of their staff had ever left to their job to do political consulting, 3) whether the chief-of-staff himself plans to run for office some day, and 4) whether a member of the staff had already run for public office.

In offices that engage in campaign lending, 75 percent had chiefs-of-staff who encouraged someone to run for public office, while only 42 percent of the top aides from nonlending offices did the same. Lending field offices were also more likely to have a staff member leave their job to set up shop as a political consultant (75 percent) as opposed to offices that do not lend (33 percent). The top aides in offices that lent out their staffs were also more politically ambitious, with 50 percent of the chiefs-of-staff in the lending offices expressing a desire to run for office someday, while *none* of the top

Table 6.7
Meeting with Staffers in Other Offices

	Total (342) %	Congress (81) %	State Senate (63) %	State Assembly (117) %	County Supervisor (15) %	City Council (66) %
Frequency of Meetings						
Daily	20	22	13	19	46	24
Weekly	27	25	13	20	46	48
Monthly	16	18	15	16	8	14
Less Often	36	36	58	44	—	14

Source: Marvick et al., *Field Office Study*, 1990.

aides from nonlending offices shared that desire. And finally, 24 percent of the offices that lent their staff to another campaign had a staff member run for a public office, while only 8 percent of the nonlenders did.

Establishing a network of followers and supporters is reinforced by the amount of contact that staffers have with each other. Table 6.7 shows the frequency of contact between staffers in different field offices.

Twenty percent report they maintain *daily* contact with staffers from other offices, and 57 percent report that they do so on a weekly basis. In fact, 42 percent of the chiefs-of-staff reported that members of their staff attend regular meetings that were organized to bring staffers from different offices together to exchange ideas, talk about problems in their districts, and gossip about politics. Many of these regular gatherings are held by various field offices on a rotating basis; other meetings are scheduled when problems arise that have an impact on a group of offices in a particular area.

Many offices reported holding meetings concerning the upcoming plans for redistricting in mid-1992. At these meetings, various redistricting plans were discussed, maps swapped, and constituent groups and neighborhoods put on the bargaining table.

CAMPAIGN COORDINATION FROM THE STATE LEGISLATURE

What has also emerged in California in not just intervention by the local elected officials, but a more centralized effort by the Republican and Democratic party caucuses in the legislature to influence electoral outcomes. An important element of this system has been the caucus-aide, whose primary duties are the running of campaigns throughout the state.[14]

The lending of expertise, whether for general campaign management or for more specialized tasks, such as fund-raising, has created networks of public officials in the legislature. Legislative leaders in both the parties have solidified party efforts in campaigns through the disbursement of campaign specialists who serve vital roles in the campaign process. In many such instances, this intervention occurs in the primaries with the party caucus identifying viable candidates, and throwing their resources behind these candidates.

> The Democratic Caucus in Sacramento will meet and say, 'Gee, there's an open seat and these are the folks who want to run.' The Caucus will then interview them up in Sacramento for the seat and they decide who the strongest candidate is. That's how it worked for my boss. She came in with all the credentials: She came in with having worked for an elected official, having been a labor union person, having all these contacts with other office holders, and knowing how to raise money. So she goes there and does her dutiful interview with all the major legislators. You have to do this, though, because it's the Caucus that sends the folks to work on the campaigns.
> —State Legislative Aide

This effort to use the Assembly caucus as a clearing house for candidates is also used by the Republicans.

> The Republican Caucus puts a lot of effort into putting staffers into those districts where they have chosen 'their' candidate. And out of the Republican Assembly Caucus—about half the people on the Caucus payroll—will shoot out and become on-site campaign people. They helped out on [my boss's] primary effort.
> —State Legislative Aide

This form of preprimary endorsement and support was one method for getting around the state restrictions that forbade preprimary endorsements by the party. The use of the legislative caucus as an electoral tool has strengthened the party's influence over those using the party label. Legislative leaders have been extremely active recruiting and supporting candidates before the primaries even begin.[15]

THE ENTERPRISE-IN-OFFICE AND
THE FORMAL PARTY APPARATUS

The idea that incumbent apparatuses are threats to the parties' role in the electoral process is difficult to reconcile with the evidence. What is the incumbent's staff competing with? If you simply define parties as bureaucratic institutions with a permanent headquarters, paid staff, and their own resources, then the parties may be said to compete ineffectively with the "enterprises-in-office." But if the parties are more than statutorily-defined institutions, then

Table 6.8
Hold a Position in the Party Organization by Office Type

	Total (342) %	Congress (81) %	State Senate (63) %	State Assembly (117) %	County Supervisor (15) %	City Council (66) %
Staffer Holds a Position in the Party	75	77	71	69	75	93

Note: Includes local and state party committees.
Source: Marvick et al., Field Office Study, 1990.

the parties encompass the incumbents' district-based organizations. Office holders are using their resources to fulfill many of the election tasks that we have come to associate with the parties.

Furthermore, political aides are very much involved in the leadership of the parties' formal apparatus. Holding formal party positions is another aspect of their job—they are the instruments by which the incumbent fulfills many of his party responsibilities. Staffers regularly attend central committee meetings as the boss's alternate in nearly one-half of these offices. But staffers are also involved in party work on their own as well. Table 6.8 details the proportion of field offices that have a staff member who holds an official position in the party. Seventy-five percent of the offices have at least one staffer who holds a formal party position, or said a different way, three-quarters of the offices had a party official on the payroll. There is little difference by office type.

The argument then becomes: if staffers are carrying out many of the party's responsibilities by holding formal positions within the party, then the political apparatus of the incumbent seems to operate in the same sphere as the party. Moreover, the political expertise and experience that staffers possess accrue to the parties because they are intertwined with the party's governing structure. As opposed to conventional wisdom, rather than making incumbents less dependent on the party, the political apparatus of the incumbent is closely intertwined with the formal party structure.

However, tensions do arise between the political aides and those working in the formal party apparatus. The tension is a classic one in party politics, pitting the professional orientations of the political staff against the amateur style of party volunteers. A Republican party chair described the tension in this way:

> It's my impression that people volunteer their time because they are concerned with a certain issue or they like a certain candidate. But

the staffers are there because it's part of their job—they have been told that they have to be there—and they are only concerned about one thing: and that is winning *that* election. It's hard to say which group is more important. I think it is important that citizens feel like they can make a difference by participating, but we also need that activity which is extended from one election to the next. This is what the legislative staffs give us.
—County Republican Party Chair

Office holders have used their electoral resources offensively to consolidate their power within the party, and, not surprisingly, they have been best placed to coordinate the electoral efforts of the party across the various levels of government. To be sure, an incumbent's political staff is there to insure the electoral success of their boss, but make no mistake, the apparatus of the incumbent makes possible the elaborate orchestration of electoral activity between actors in the party's structure. The field staff is a powerful political resource that can be deployed to create linkages with new candidates attempting to win office for the first time, with office holders running for a higher seat, and with incumbents attempting to retain the seat they have. The incumbents' enterprises-in-office, and more specifically the linkages created and maintained between them, are reshaping the political process in profound ways. The field operation of elected officials forms the core of the modern political party, and the incumbent's personal staff is the parties' patronage workforce.

7

Mini-Machines

Constituency Service

Problems are problems. Most constituents don't care if it's a
local, state, or federal problem. And in the end, neither do
we. The important thing is that, when they call, we're here
to help them.

—State Legislative Aide

While the electoral activities of the district operation are purposely
screened from public scrutiny, the field office goes to great lengths to
advertise its wares as a troubleshooter for citizens' problems with government.
Constituency service is its core function. There is evidence that strongly suggests that legislators' focus on constituency service is responsible for the rise
of candidate-centered voting and for the entrenchment of members of Congress
in "safe" electoral districts (Mayhew 1974; Fiorina 1977; Cain, et al. 1987).

The politics of favoritism is a necessary part of this process. Bringing
public goods to the district and acting as a troubleshooter for his constituents
allow an incumbent to establish an interdependent relationship with his constituents. For the citizen, politics is transformed into personal ties with the
incumbent. For the incumbent, favors yield tangible electoral dividends. The
way Merton described the urban machine several decades ago still rings true
today:

> The political machine does not regard the electorate as an amor-
> phous, undifferentiated mass of voters. With a keen sociological
> intuition, the machine recognizes that the voter is a person living in
> a specific neighborhood, with specific personal problems and per-
> sonal wants. Public issues are abstract and remote; private prob-
> lems are extremely concrete and immediate. It is not through the
> generalized appeal to large public concerns that the machine operates,
> but through the direct, quasi-feudal relationships between local

99

representatives of the machine and voters in their neighborhood. Elections are won in the precinct. (1957, 74)

Though the longevity of incumbents in office may, in part, be traced to the increasing ability of members of Congress and state legislators to forge ties with their constituents, this does not preclude the existence of a party structure, even a highly centralized one. The ability of incumbents to gain a measure of electoral security through the *servicing* of their constituents frees the incumbent to pursue influence in other areas. "Safe" incumbents have more resources that can be used to establish and maintain linkages with other actors in the party network. District operations allow incumbents to gain access to the raw materials to fulfill this goal.

FIXING PROBLEMS: CASEWORK

We act as a liaison between constituents and the government—at all levels. We grease the tracks and smooth out the problems. Everybody has to deal with government and I see it as our job to make those contacts come out in the constituents favor. We may solve 40 problems a day. That might not sound like a lot, but multiply that times 365 days a year and you're looking at a lot of support. Not just from them, but from their families and friends too.
—Congressional Aide

A primary function of the district apparatus is to intervene when citizens are having problems with government. This is a subset of constituency service that deals with dispensing particularized benefits to individual citizens. However, casework involves more that just helping citizens with problems with a government agency. Requests for assistance can range from information about pending legislation to getting a constituent's utilities reconnected. The amount of staff resources devoted to individual casework varied from office to office, though most offices reported that they spend less than 50 percent of their time dealing with individual constituents. Table 7.1 shows the amount of time the field office spent handling individual cases.

State Assembly offices report spending significantly less time doing individual casework, with 73 percent spending less than one-half of their time responding to individual requests for assistance. Congressional offices, on the other hand, are much more involved in dealing with complaints from individual citizens, with 59 percent spending more than one-half of their time with individual constituents. Both State Assembly and congressional staffers explained this discrepancy by pointing to the greater visibility of congressional offices. Constituents are more likely to be aware of their member of Congress than their state representative. Constituents will often contact

Table 7.1
Percentage of the Staff Activity Spent on Casework

	Total (50) %	Democrat (30) %	Republican (20) %	Congress (22) %	Assembly (28) %
Time Spent on Casework					
0 to 50%	58	57	60	41	73
50 to 100%	42	43	40	59	27

Source: *Chief-of-Staff Interviews*, 1992.

the wrong office, asking for assistance from a state level office in a federal matter or contacting a congressional office about a problem with a state agency.[1]

For many constituents, the decision about whom to call with a problem is often based on their past experience in receiving aid. If they received a favorable hearing from a particular incumbent, they will often call the same incumbent's office despite the source of the problem. Eighty-one percent of all the offices report that they receive a large amount of "repeat business" from satisfied constituents. As one state legislative aide described:

We have our regulars—people that call us about everything—from their gas bill to a problem with the Department of Motor Vehicles. I have this one constituent—I really like this old woman. I'm the only one that she ever talks to—I'm it; it's me and her neighbor. She calls me every single day, even when I'm busy.

Another source of repeat business is constituents passing on reports of their success to family and friends. The successful resolution of a case is one of the best forms of advertisement for the field office.[2]

A majority of the individual cases handled by the field office deal with citizen contacts with government agencies of one type or another. Congressional staffers report that 80 percent of their individual cases deal with some type of government agency and State Assembly staffers reported that 65 percent of casework involves problems with a government agency.[3] Much of this intervention for constituents involves bringing the problem to the attention of the staffer's key contacts in various governmental agencies. The staffer represents the constituent's interests in a matter that may involve some agency discretion. Knowing the ins and outs of the bureaucratic system is one advantage that staffers can offer their constituents. Most are unfamiliar with the complexities of the agency's organization and its decision-making structure.

Table 7.2
Aspects of Job Liked by Field Staffers

	Total (342) %
Aspects of Job Liked by Staffers	
Helping Citizens Coping with Red Tape	81
Learning about the Local Community	75
Influencing Specific Government Policies	58
Seeing How Legislators Do Their Job	55
Getting Skills Needed in a Political Career	31
Contacts that Help a Career in Politics	26

Note: Multiple responses.
Source: Marvick et al., *Field Office Study*, 1990.

Much of the help that the field office provides is straightening out problems after a constituent has contacted the agency and is getting little response.
Their case may be tangled in "red tape" or the complexity of the matter defies
an easy solution. These are problems that many constituents have spent
months attempting to solve, and they finally turn to the legislative field office
to appeal for help. The message that many offices attempt to communicate to
their constituents is that they should contact the office first.[4]

This desire to help constituents with government agencies is reflected in
Table 7.2. Staffers were asked what they liked about their jobs, and topping
the list was helping constituents "cope with red tape" with 81 percent indicating this reason. Close behind was "learning about the local community"
with 75 percent.

Veteran staffers have noticed a change in constituency casework. Not
only has the volume been increasing over the last decade, but the constituents'
attitudes about the role of the field office have also changed. Many staffers
reported that constituents often contact the field office *before* contacting the
government agency to use the congressional or state legislative office as added
clout in their interaction with bureaucrats. A twenty-year veteran for a member of Congress described the change this way:

> Twenty years ago, I was a one girl office and now it takes eight
> what I did by myself. The increase has a lot to do with the amount
> of government intervention in people's lives. In the past, people
> tried to deal with the agencies themselves, and when they weren't
> getting anywhere, they would contact us. Now, many constituents
> contact us before they ever make contact with a particular agency.

There just has been an increase in the willingness of the average person to call their congressman about a problem—any problem.

The benefit of constituency casework to the incumbent is difficult to empirically demonstrate. However, the sheer volume of aid given constituents suggests that an incumbent's desire to provide good constituency service does not go unnoticed by the constituents. First, it is an activity in which the constituent has a tangible basis for measuring incumbent performance. The favors performed by incumbents are not abstract issues dealing with public policy, nor are they fuzzy pronouncements about issues remote to the experience of the average voter. These are personal problems that are salient and close to the constituent's experience. Second, it is an activity for which the incumbent's name is firmly attached. There is no ambiguity about who solved the problem, and thus no ambiguity about who to reward for solving it. All of the field staffs know this, and they dispense favors to the incumbent's gain. A congressional staffer described the process this way:

> People come in and shake hands with the congressman—he's very good, he's very personable. He talks with each one individually. And if they have a problem, we walk behind taking notes, so that we can resolve the problem. They will come back in on Open House and thank him personally. We took all of the notes and handled it for them, but as far as that constituent is concerned, the congressman did it for him personally.[5]

CROSS-JURISDICTIONAL ACTIVITY

In most of the literature, casework is defined as assistance to citizens in their dealings with agencies congruent with the incumbent's level of governmental responsibility (Fox and Hammond 1977; Kofmehl 1977; Mayhew 1974). In practice, however, casework often involves intervention by an incumbent's staff at every level of government. Table 7.3 examines this cross-jurisdictional nature of contact by the field offices.

As the table shows, there are many cross-jurisdictional inquiries made by the legislative field offices. Sixty-eight percent of the congressional offices intervened in cases dealing with a state agency, 59 percent of them with agencies at the county level, and 36 percent with the city. Similarly, 73 percent of the State Assembly field offices made inquiries on behalf of constituents with federal agencies, 50 percent with the county and 58 percent with the city. Much of this cross-jurisdiction activity is prompted by the overlapping nature of constituent problems. For example, constituents who are having difficulty with Social Security may also need state medical assistance. Although the cross-jurisdictional intervention by the

Table 7.3
Cross-Jurisdictional Activity

	Total (50) %	Democrat (30) %	Republican (20) %	Congress (22) %	Assembly (28) %
Agency Level					
Federal	85	89	80	100	73
State	85	93	75	68	100
County	54	71	30	59	50
City	48	64	25	36	58

Note: Multiple responses.
Source: Chief-of-Staff Interviews, 1992.

field office occurs for a variety of cases, the most common cases were those dealing with welfare or unemployment.

Some offices receiving requests for assistance that lie outside their jurisdiction simply refer the constituent to their representative at the appropriate level of government. However, by far the most common practice was to accept the case at least making the initial contact with the agency, remaining the constituents' contact person.[6]

> Our motto is after Harry Truman: 'The buck stops here.' It makes no difference whether it's a city problem or state. We don't treat it as such. When they come to us, they usually have exhausted all their avenues, so we take anything on.
> —Congressional Aide

Though hardly a common practice, several offices mentioned that they took on cross-jurisdictional cases because the representative at that level of government was from the opposing party. Many staffers frankly thought that they could do a better job handling the constituent's problem than their partisan rivals, while simultaneously garnering constituent support that would otherwise accrue to their opponents.[7]

This form of competition for constituency cases would probably be more common if the areas in the study were not so one-party dominant. In Los Angeles and Orange counties, congressional, State Senate, and Assembly offices cluster in the same area.

Some cases not only lie outside their jurisdiction, but they may not even deal with a government agency at all. The field offices intervene in labor disputes between employers and employees, in cases between insurance companies and policyholders, and, though staffers are prohibited from giving legal advice, many staffers do and will "represent" some constituents in legal cases. Although this type of intervention in the private sphere comprised only 10 percent of congressional and 16 percent of State Assembly casework, it is significant nevertheless.[8]

The district offices frequently become embroiled in local and community issues—many of which exceed the jurisdictional boundaries of their level of government. Many aides revealed that they enjoy considerable autonomy in deciding which side of a local issue the office will support. In two separate interviews, aides reported that they organized efforts that forced the relocation of a prison in their communities. Others said that they helped to determine the outcome of local school board decisions, saved historical landmarks, altered city bus routes, changed billing practices at local utility companies, and prevented various kinds of commercial development. By virtue of their strategic location in the district and access to information and expertise, political aides have an influence on the direction of local policy.

CONTACTS

Staffers are effective as liaisons between citizens and government because they make the gears of government turn for their constituents. This is partially derived from the prestige of the office and the legislator's name that can be used to open doors in the agency.[9] However, many staffers specifically deemphasized this way of influencing agency decisions. More often, staffers rely on contacts that they have maintained over the years to influence key decisionmakers, both in and out of government. The responsiveness of the agency cannot be guaranteed by just using the incumbent's name. Access does not necessarily mean influence.[10] Although most federal and state agencies have legislative liaison officers who work directly with the offices making inquires on behalf of constituents, it is often the personal contacts with members of the agency that provide the most fruitful avenue for solving tricky problems.

> After twelve years of dealing with the agencies, you build up a relationship with the people in those offices. Some of them have been around as long as I have. It becomes a mutual kind of thing—everyone does favors for everybody else.
> —Congressional Aide

Some staffers used to work in government agencies and they continue to maintain those contacts after leaving the agency. Having these people to go to with problems are important reasons for the amount of influence staffers have.[11]

Official channels for problem resolution are sometimes rejected for more expedient channels. Contacts are made with specific people because the field office has established a successful record of solving problems with that person. Some staffers are even assigned certain agencies because they have especially good relations with a particular person.

> You tend to develop relationships with the people in the different agencies. We have a staffer who just clicks with someone on the Franchise Tax Board. Things just got straightened out—it wasn't that anything was done differently; it was that they managed to understand each other and got things straightened out.
> —State Legislative Aide

Knowing the rules and becoming an expert in that area is another element for having successful contacts with the agencies. Speaking the same language was a common theme mentioned by staffers.[12] The development of contacts also bears fruit in terms of reciprocal contacts by members of the agency. Before decisions are made, the agency will often contact the field office to let them know of an impending problem or decision.[13]

DEVELOPING A DISTRICT "FEEL"

A large part of the job of the district operation is to establish and maintain contact with various constituents and groups in the district. The development of a "feel" for the district is something that many staffers said was a prerequisite for doing a good job. Most staffers reported that they were familiar with the area before taking the job. Table 7.4 shows the level of district knowledge of staffers before they took their position with the incumbent.

Forty-two percent report that they knew the area "very well." This is not surprising given the length of time that many have lived in the area. Staffers have lived an average of 12 years in their district, and an average of 30 years in California. This all displays a significant level of presence in the area.

While field offices differ greatly in specialization, it is possible to characterize some staffers as field workers, principally attending public events in assigned areas of the district. Their task is to focus on active groups in the community, acting as a proxy for the elected legislator.

The staffers were asked how often each month they attended public events as part of their staff job. Apart from events like speeches, testimonial dinners, forums, receptions, funerals, weddings, and so forth, each district—indeed, each community within a district—has a host of groups that expect the presence of the office at their meetings. On average, about 13 meetings per month are attended by each field staffer. Nearly one-half the offices assign a staffer to maintain contact with various groups in the district. This ranged from Republican office holders in Orange County who assigned field representatives to work with large Vietnamese groups in the district to

Table 7.4
District Knowledge Before Taking Job

	Total (342) %
District Knowledge	
Very Familiar with District	42
Somewhat Familiar with District	33
Only a Little Familiar with District	15
Not at All Familiar with District	10

Source: Marvick et al., *Field Office Study*, 1990.

Democratic office holders on the Eastside of Los Angeles who worked with Latino groups and organizations. For one member of Congress, a field representative's *sole* responsibility entailed maintaining contact with his district's large Jewish community by attending meetings, speaking at dinners, and writing congratulatory letters for weddings, bar mitzvahs, and job promotions.

One chief-of-staff for a state Assembly office required that her field representatives know every business, church, and organization in the member's district. The field representatives had to identify the location of each of these on a map and "pass" a quiz (requiring a perfect score) before they were allowed to venture into the community.

Clearly, over the last several decades, incumbents have been more inclined to pour greater resources into their district operations with the purpose of garnering electoral support. However, this strategy yields other benefits as well. Beyond simply securing support at the polls, the community itself can be used as a resource, if cultivated properly. Tapping into various segments of the community is a useful device for mobilizing support for the incumbent's issue-specific goals. Maintaining good constituency liaison insures that when the incumbent needs the community's help they can be used to put pressure on various government agencies and other legislators. One congressional aide, after describing their successful campaign to reverse an agency's policy, believed that their key to success was the mobilization of the activist core in the district:

> All segments of the community can be tapped. You just have to figure out what it is that you want from them. But it has to be an honest exchange. They will want to know what's in it for them.
> —Congressional Aide

Building this potential requires a keen awareness of the various interests in the district and effective communication of the incumbent's goals. Part of this process requires opening the office as a focal point for the community's interest groups. These groups use the resources of the office to accomplish their own ends.[14]

One way to cultivate support from interest groups is to actively seek out problems. Rather than sitting back and letting problems come to the field office, incumbents and their staffers spend an enormous amount of time searching for problems to solve and groups to represent. The staffers themselves will often take the lead in organizing certain groups such as homeowners, local businesses, and ethnic groups. This activist approach increases the clout of the office and diffuses problems before they occur.[15]

SURVEILLANCE

A common pattern among the field offices was to divide the district into geographically recognizable units for assigning responsibility. The same field staffer would normally handle all the casework, social events, and political problems in a given municipality or community. Dividing the work by localities meant that each field staffer had to be versatile and had to know how to handle the same kinds of bureaucratic problems, rather than have one person who specialized in social services or IRS cases. Treating each locality as a semi-autonomous social, economic, and political community was virtually the only way to effectively monitor developments in a given area.

The desire to develop an intimate knowledge of different parts of the district drives the organization of the field office itself. Because district problems are conceptualized in geographic terms, field representatives are assigned the problems in specific areas of the district. Table 7.5 shows how the field offices organize their field representatives.

Seventy-seven percent adopt the strategy of assigning field representatives to recognizable geographical units within the district. Thirteen percent assigned field staffers to cover certain political or social issues, and 10 percent had field representatives cover the district as a whole without regard to geopolitical divisions within the district. The difference between congressional and State Assembly offices is striking. Only 59 percent of the congressional offices adopted the geographic strategy, while 92 percent of the Assembly offices did. A chief-of-staff for a member of the Assembly described how new staffers have to learn all aspects of the district:

> Part of the learning curve is knowing the agencies, the schools, the churches, and putting it into a mental directory. We have a map of the district; they have to identify where everything is in the district, whether it be the Asian community, whether it be Eastside businesses,

Table 7.5
District Problems and the Assignment of Field Representatives

	Total (50) %	Democrat (30) %	Republican (20) %	Congress (22) %	Assembly (28) %
Assignment Strategy					
Geographically	77	71	85	59	92
Politically / Socially	13	21	–	23	4
Districtwide	10	7	15	18	4

Source: *Chief-of-Staff Interviews*, 1992.

up to and including churches and bakeries, wherever [the member of the Assembly] has gone out.

All of these represent different strategies for managing constituency problems. Each is also a different contact orientation, a way of designing the field office to make the most of its contacts with the various agencies, groups, and constituents in the district environment. Effective management of information requires that field representatives establish and maintain personalized contacts with key people in the district. It is part of the surveillance function of the district operation. To identify potential allies and opposition within the district, most staffers conclude that nothing replaces making face-to-face contacts with certain individuals and groups.

This level of district scrutiny arguably pales in comparison with the level of contact achieved by the urban machines of the past. However, the level of contact with constituents, especially organized and active constituents, is impressive.

You know, I grew up in Chicago—now that was a different system. They had graft and corruption and all that. The precinct captain would know things—I mean really know the details about the community. He knew that the guy down the street had three kids who were heading off to college and that money was getting pretty tight for him. We can't cover the district to that extent. But we do try to keep tabs on what's important to the community—even individual constituents.

Building constituent support extends beyond a vote-getting potential. Having a well-organized district apparatus means that the field office has established and maintains a stable core of informants in the community who apprise the field operation about local problems and developments.

The beauty of doing field work is that when all of a sudden the
people you met are calling you and telling you what's happening—
then you're not running around trying to find out what's happening,
people are doing it for you.
—State Legislative Aide

The district operation goes to great lengths to open channels with the
various groups within the district. Many staffers are assigned to be a liaison
with many different groups, attending their meetings regularly, with the goal
of collecting information about their activities and representing their boss's
interests among the activist community. The field representatives, in particular, seek out opportunities to mix and mingle with the leaders of each community. This allows them a twofold opportunity. The first is to let constituents
see that "their representative is visible in the community; that he is there if
they need any help." The second opportunity is "to learn about developments
in the community."[16] Many staffers stressed the importance of this surveillance activity as a way of getting ahead of problems before they become
unmanageable.[17]

Attendance at local events and organized meetings not only provides the
office the chance to hear what issues are important in the district, but it also
gives the incumbent the opportunity to advertise his services. Most state and
congressional field offices employ at least one field representative whose primary function is to serve as an immediate link between constituents and the
field apparatus. A great deal of the time is spent representing the incumbent
at the regular meetings throughout the district. The variety of meetings is
staggering. And each allows the incumbent to advertise his wares as a problem-
solver, a conscientious representative, and a community organizer.

Most staffers contend that, though the bulk of their contact with constituents is either over the phone or through the mail, maintaining personal
contacts with constituents is an important element of the job. Many staffers
stressed the need to meet their constituents in person and through regular
community meetings.[18]

Some offices had operations manuals that described in detail the surveillance activity of the field office. To get a better idea of this process, a
portion of an operations manual for a member of the State Assembly is
reproduced in Table 7.6.

COOPERATION WITH OTHER STAFFS

Government projects often have multiple sources of funding; industries are
regulated by both state and federal agencies; and problems affecting constituents can touch all levels of government. Cooperation between the field offices

Table 7.6
Operations Manual for a Member of the State Assembly

A. Community leader forums, advisory groups (i.e., business, civic)
  1. Semi-annual meeting to discuss legislation and legislative concepts that member might introduce. Insure participation of Political Action Committee representatives
  2. Periodic mailings to advisory groups and where appropriate all professional members regarding legislation and activities important to their specific concerns

B. Community activities
  1. Annual report by member to service clubs, school boards, city councils, Board of Supervisors, Chamber of Commerce, etc.
  2. Periodic attendance of same by Administrative Assistant or Field Representamtive
  3. Regular mailings of legislative information, newsletters

C. Single-issue interest group members
  1. Identify members of single-issue interest groups (i.e., anti-gun control, pro-capital punishment, pro-life, anti-crime, etc.)
  2. Periodic mailings to each group's members showing Assemblymanís leadership in Sacramento on their specific issue of concern
  3. Regular mailings or legislative informational newsletter

D. Identify and communicate in-person and through the mail with members of community groups (i.e., senior citizens, youth groups, cultural organizations, etc.)

E. Regular meetings with key officials in district (i.e., councilmen, law enforcement officials, district attorneys, etc.)

F. Periodic visits to district facilities (i.e., plants, mills, hospitals, prisons, etc.)

G. High school and college campus visitations and speeches

H. Make regular phone calls to voters (20 to 30 per week) directly from registration lists assigned to strategic geographical priorities

I. Town hall meetings

J. Special programs
  1. Club officers leavings office
  2. Eagle scouts
  3. Voter registration activities
  4. Key community events or achievements
  5. Birthday card program
  6. 50th wedding anniversary
  7. Election or appointment of new club officers
  8. Scholarships, retirement, promotions
  9. Block grants, community programs
  10. Civic awards

is a strategy for dealing with these divisions in government. An important feature of this process involves combining the unique forms of expertise that each staff brings to the collaborative process. Although field offices display a remarkable propensity to work with all government agencies, they are experts on the agencies within their jurisdiction. They bring their contacts into the process. An example of this is explained by a congressional staffer:

> We know what's going on at the federal and at the local level, but you can't be an expert at all levels, so therefore, you have to call on other staff members and they have to call on us. So that's why that there is such good rapport with other staff members.

Coordinated action is often promoted by common complaints arising from several districts. In one such case, the local IRS office was closing businesses that were behind in their taxes. Several offices banded together to arbitrate on behalf of the businesses in their respective districts:

> We were getting some complaints about this guy in the IRS, so we rounded up all of the chiefs-of-staff in the area. We had our own strategy meeting to figure out how to approach this thing. We were going to play hard-ball with these guys.
> —Congressional Aide

Table 7.7 shows the proportion of field offices that report coordinating their constituency projects with other offices.

Probably the most important condition promoting coordinated action between the field offices is when they have common constituencies—the commonality is created by the overlapping nature of the districts. Congressional districts will generally have two Assembly districts within their boundaries, creating opportunities to tackle problems affecting common constituencies. Thus, geographical proximity promotes the coordination of activity between different field offices.

Having common constituency groups also promotes cooperation. This often has a geographical component. Latino and African-American groups are clustered in specific areas of the County. However, this would not explain the coordination of the staffs in noncontiguous districts. Regular meetings are sometimes held in this regard. Most of the various ethnic constituencies in Los Angeles County are represented in this fashion. According to one congressional staffer:

> We meet quarterly with any Chiefs-of-Staff that have a large African-American constituency. We involve the Mayor's office. So, for example, the congressional office will host and they may want to talk about some federal issue that they think may have an impact

Table 7.7
Coordination of Constituency Projects

	Total (50) %	Democrat (30) %	Republican (20) %	Congress (22) %	Assembly (28) %
Worked with Other Offices					
At Least One Office	96	100	90	96	96
Congressional	71	75	65	64	77
State Senate	69	82	55	64	77
State Assembly	69	68	70	82	58
Local Offices	58	61	55	64	54

Note: Multiple responses.
Source: *Chief-of-Staff Interviews*, 1992.

on the state. One issue that we talked about a few months ago was reapportionment because that will affect all of us.

THE FIELD OFFICE, CONSTITUENTS, AND THE PARTY

Incumbents at the local, state, and national levels have established district-based operations that operate in much the same way as the urban political machines. It is with the same sense of intuition that the incumbent's apparatus link citizens with the government. The structure of the institution may look nothing like the urban machines of old, but the politics that animate them have not changed. The district-based apparatus provides access to government; it has influence with local, state, and federal bureaucrats; and it has the added clout of combining its efforts with the field offices of other incumbents in the area.

But it does not end here; helping individual citizens is only part of the process. The district operation also acts as a liaison between the organized interests in a district and government, whether these are ethnic, economic, or political. Here, representation shades into promotion as the district office is used to advance the group's interests. In exchange, these groups can be used by the incumbent as a resource to increase his own influence, not only in the legislative game, but also his influence in electoral contests at the local level. The incumbent's apparatus is not only lodged in a network of other incumbents seeking influence in the political arena, but it is also lodged in a network of politically active groups seeking the same kind of influence.

8

The Entitlement Party

How can we compete? Incumbents get their own personal
army—one not only devoted to them, but to whoever else
they decide to support.

—County Republican Party Chair

In 1972, David Broder's book, *The Party's Over*, represented the near consensus among academics and journalists concerning the crisis in party politics. A decade later, scholars were arguing that the parties-as-organizations were
making a comeback. The parties, especially at the national level, were adapting
to the requirements of modern politics. Both parties developed institutional
strategies and resources to fight off challenges from nonparty competitors in
campaigns. According to this orthodoxy of party renewal, the period of party
weakness was only a temporary setback as the parties regrouped and reinvigorated their institutions. The parties died and then were resurrected, or so the
story goes. But is this the way it really happened? This interpretation of party
development has been accepted with little scrutiny. What we failed to realize is
that the development of formal institutions at the national and state levels is
new, not a process necessarily linked to the supposedly moribund institutions
of the past. The orthodoxy of party renewal argues that America's weak parties
(those devastated by early twentieth-century reforms and more recent technological advances) reemerged, capturing some of their old glory. Thus, the parties
as formal organizations were revitalized.

However, it is important to keep in mind that this statutorily defined
party was merely an early twentieth-century device used by reformers to
wrest control of the party away from professional politicians and away from
a party that already existed. Hoping to gain a foothold in the party, reformers
mandated that, to be recognized by the state, political parties had to conform
to a set of institutional requirements. The rise of a modern campaign-oriented
apparatus at the national and state levels of the parties did not restore a pre-
existing structure; they are fundamentally new.

Closer to reality is that the parties in America never had formal institutions worth resurrecting. They simply did not need them. Why, then, are we wed to this image of the party? To see how this orthodoxy emerged, it is necessary to bring together (as others have done) what were two separate research streams in American politics.

The thesis of party decline first emerged from the studies on voting behavior. The decades following the first National Election Study were marked by a measurable decline in party identifiers for both of the parties. Party scholars began searching for plausible explanations to account for this decline. One of these was that the parties-as-organizations were deteriorating and citizens responded by assigning a diminished role for the party in the political arena. Political scientists had noticed this too. The literature on parties was full of accounts about the passing of the old machines. And for American party scholars this form had become the quintessential American political party. With this party benchmark in hand, political scientists determined that the disappearance of certain institutional features meant that contemporary parties had suffered an inexorable decline. The decline in party identification became yet another piece of evidence confirming the withering of political parties in this country.

But the truth of the matter is that, while the search for highly organized party institutions came up empty during the 1950s and 1960s, they were never there to begin with. The old machines that found a place in our political lore were never typical of American party organizations, nor did the formal apparatus ever represent the real party. In most places and at most times, political parties in America have maintained skeletal institutions. This is as true today as it was 100 years ago. To capture office, which is what political parties are good for, parties in American never needed the European-style organizations. American political parties formed around strong candidates, courthouse gangs, and loose associations of interest groups. To do otherwise was to do more than was necessary to win office.

Meanwhile, political scientists have lamented the passing of something that probably never existed in America. We have opted for a highly stylized view of what political parties are in this country, ignoring the historical and contemporary realities that give political parties their particular form. While this book argues that what has emerged in this country is a new party organization, in truth there is nothing particularly new about it. The parties in Los Angeles conform to a time-honored form of organization in this country. What is different is the way it has been accomplished. The professionalization of state and national legislatures has given the parties new resources to do what they have always done. The specific way that influence is aggregated may be different, but the loose institutional arrangements maintained in Los Angeles look much the same as they did in the past. It is a story of structural continuity and resource innovation.

THE REPROFESSIONALIZATION OF PARTY POLITICS

There are two parties out there. There is 'us' and there is the 'party of the office holders.' We, the party representatives, unfortunately have little to do with who actually wins or losses an election. The real power in elections resides with those who hold office.
—County Democratic Party Chair

The previous quotation describes more than the status quo, a description of the difference between those who hold power and those who want it. It illustrates a fundamental change in American politics: the *re*-professionalization of party politics. The County Chair, like many of those who hold positions in the formal apparatus, is an amateur devoting what is left over in his professional life to the pursuit of politics. By contrast, those who work within the office holder's enterprise-in-office devote their professional lives *to* politics. They are in every sense of the term professional politicians.

At one time in American politics, the political parties represented the only professionalism in the public sphere. Nearly a century ago, proponents of "good government" vigorously fought this professionalism, arguing that public life was being displaced by professional politicians. These participants were lifelong political practitioners who reaped the rewards that the system offered. The institution worked as a party because it provided a channel for individual ambition, allowed for collaboration between fragmented institutional arenas, and traded public goods for continued support in office.

Reformers attacked the spoils system, the instrument for using patronage, as a corrupt and inefficient mode of governance. The reforms succeeded in making politics less corrupt, and perhaps less party-oriented. By the 1950s, most local governments were inhabited with prominent citizens and those who had made careers outside public life. "Citizen-run" legislative bodies met infrequently so that office holders could pursue careers outside the political arena. The day-to-day affairs of the cities were run by another kind of professional, city managers and bureaucrats, and emphasized rational decision-making and neutral competence over politics.

Until the 1960s, state legislatures were similarly "citizen" institutions throughout the United States, with most of them in session no more than three months of the year. The legislators were farmers, lawyers, local merchants, and others willing to take the time from private pursuits to devote themselves to the chore of making public policy.

Congress has not been an amateur body in the same way as state legislatures and city governments; service in Congress has been a full-time job for most of this century (Polsby 1968). Still, its members were not careerists in the modern sense; most did not pursue a lifetime career in Congress.

The system of citizen politics that existed in this country was abolished when we raised the pay and upgraded the resources of legislative bodies to the point where people would want to serve in them full-time. This was done for a variety of reasons, not all concerning a desire to increase the partisan nature of the institution. In Congress, professionalization—upgrading committee staffs and creating centralized research units—was perhaps initiated to offset the expanding influence of the presidency or the bureaucracy. Likewise, many legislators may have initiated reforms to professionalize their legislative bodies, to challenge the power of the governor or to become more modern, effective governing institutions. For whatever reason, legislative resources are not by their nature nonpartisan. The transition from nonpartisan to partisan staff appears to occur quite rapidly (Weberg 1988).

The citizen was also pushed out by expanding the scope of government itself, to the point where the old amateur institutions could not handle the volume of constituency demands (Fiorina 1977). It seems to follow that the continuing growth in the scope, complexity, and impersonality of institutional life would produce greater need for politicians to mediate between individuals and the government. The growth of the welfare state has not diminished this need but increased it, and presumably offers opportunities for helping citizens get what they want from government. Helping citizens deal with government in this context is usually thought to be a matter of advice: where to go, whom to see, and what to say. But field offices in Los Angeles combine advice to citizens with pressure on public officials. The office holder's goal is to incur the maximum obligation from his constituents, and merely providing information is not as big a favor as helping to produce the desired outcome.

In a very real sense, we have come full circle since the nineteenth century. The professionalism of that day was not that different from the way it is today. And, also like the past, this professionalization has implications for the political parties. The link between professionalism and the parties is an important one. Professionalism is simply how ambition is expressed in our system. As long as we have a system that allows individuals to live both "for" and "off" politics, political parties will naturally form in this country. Professionalism creates viable grooming and sponsoring machinery for those seeking a professional life in politics or the ultimate goal of holding public office. Professionalism sustains the activity of those participants as they compete within the political arena. And professionalism creates incentives for collaborative efforts in government.

What emerges from these developments is a political party. All the necessary ingredients are here: attractive, reasonably well-paying legislative salaries and staff positions, a viable recruitment machinery for the politically ambitious, ample resources to extend one's influence, and hungry citizens who demand that their legislator act as a "go-between" with a monolithic and uncaring bureaucracy. What has emerged is an "entitlement" party that has access to resources automatically, by just showing up. These resources differ from those a century ago in one major respect: they are entirely respectable (Marvick 1990).

The growth of the enterprise-in-office for America's elected officials is reshaping the political terrain. The parties are still confronting the same maze of offices at the local, state, and national levels making centralization of the party's aims through a party bureaucracy at best difficult. Institutional coherence in the modern party relies on loose structural ties, rather than an overarching party bureaucracy. This is why traditional efforts to apply bureaucratic or organizational theories to capture the structure of the parties have failed. The parties were never highly structured institutions, and the modern party is no exception. Nevertheless, the modern party can marshal a consistent level of political activity and amass a formidable array of resources. Of course, these look different from those used by parties of the past, but they help the modern party achieve many of the same goals.

Appendix A

This appendix provides additional information about how the research was conducted. The questionnaires used in the survey are also provided in this appendix.

THE CHIEFS-OF-STAFF

Sample

The sample of offices in the study included all of the congressional and State Assembly field offices in Los Angeles County, for a total of fifty offices. The chiefs-of-staff were identified by the *Congressional Staff Directory and the California Political Almanac* and were sent a brief letter requesting an interview with them at some future date. I followed up these written requests with phone calls requesting a specific meeting time and place. I encountered two difficulties with scheduling the interviews. The first was that it was necessary to convince them that I was who I said that I was. Many political aides wanted to make certain that I was not a muckraking journalist looking for politically embarrassing information.

The second difficulty was that a chief-of-staff working in a field office has very little free time, especially for someone such as me who appeared to be offering little in return for their time. Some interviews took over two months to set up. In all, I made over 300 phone calls including the initial contact and numerous follow up calls. Out of the 51 offices in my original interview pool, only one turned me down outright, and I interviewed the remaining 50 political aides in my sample. I suspect that some finally granted interviews just to be rid of me, though others seemed quite eager to speak with me.

All of the staffers were promised anonymity; they would not be identified by name, the office holder that they worked for, or district number.

Conducting the Interviews

After selecting the offices that were to be included in the sample, the first dilemma that I faced was whether to record the interviews. On the one hand, recording the interviews would insure that I would have an accurate account of the interview—one that did not depend on my faulty memory. On the other hand, the presence of a tape recorder would perhaps jeopardize the veracity of the replies, especially when the gray area of campaigning was raised. I opted to record the interviews based on several factors. First, I had never conducted interviews like this before, except a set of interviews that I conducted to get a feel for the process. Also, having to pay attention to what was being said, asking good follow-up questions, controlling the pace of the interview, and then producing an accurate account of the interview seemed an arduous task to say the least. Recording the interviews solved many of these problems. Second, having recorded interviews not only allowed me to present verbatim quotes, but this also gave me the opportunity to go back and listen to interviews as I gathered further information. This was an invaluable tool. Answers to questions that seemed to carry little significance early in the process became very important later. The duration of the interviews averaged 65 minutes; however, some lasted for more than 2 hours.

After setting up the interview with the office holder's aide, I made a point of confirming my appointment a day before the appointment time. Many interviews were made a month in advance and my contact often forgot that I was coming. On a couple of occasions, the chief-of-staff had left town and these interviews had to be rescheduled.

The issue of recording the interviews was broached when I was ushered into the aide's office. I would explain that the interviews would remain confidential and that recording them was simply a more accurate alternative to taking notes. In the end, out of fifty interviews only two respondents refused to be recorded—both were aides for members of Congress.

I would describe the interviews as semistructured. By this I mean that I had a definite set of questions that I was prepared to ask in the interview itself. However, when the respondents would veer off into new territory, I would gladly tag along, fully exploring the topic that they raised before returning to the structured format. I made it a point to never cut off an answer, letting the interview take its own shape. Some *answers* lasted one-half an hour or more. Most took great pains to describe in detail their opinions and their activities. Most, if not all, of the respondents liked talking about themselves and their job.

The semistructured nature of the interview produced a wealth of information. Where possible the interviews were coded to be used in statistical analysis. The open-ended questions yielded a wealth of qualitative information about the nature of the district apparatus. When quotes are used, they are direct quotes taken from the recording of the interviews.

I also compiled detailed notes immediately after each interview. In these notes I would describe the office setting, the pace and activity of the office, and other impressions that I felt were significant. In addition, I rated the interviewee for frankness, willingness to talk, and how truthful I thought their replies had been.

Most interviews concluded with a tour of the office. On these tours, I gathered additional information about the operation of the field office. I met (and interviewed) other members of the staff, or even the legislator if he or she was in the office that day. Sometimes I was allowed to "hang out" and observe the staffers' interaction with constituents or just listen in on phone conversations.

THE CONSULTANTS

Sample

The decision of whom to interview was a simple matter. I decided to interview those consultants who worked for the office holders in my office holder pool. The consultants were identified by the state and federal campaign spending reports filed by the candidates that identify all expenditures made by the candidate, including the names and professions of those who were paid. Due to time constraints, I could not interview all forty consultants, so I therefore drew a random sample of thirty consultants to be interviewed. The consultants were also sent a brief letter requesting an interview that was followed up with a phone call to set a specific time and date. All thirty agreed to be interviewed. The consultants were also promised anonymity.

Conducting the Interviews

My primary enemy in gaining access to the consultants was that they are stingy with their time. And unlike the field staffers, they cannot always be pinned down in a particular office location. The interviews, therefore, took place in their offices (when they had one), in their homes, or in various public places, such as restaurants. As with the chiefs-of-staff, the interviews were recorded, and no consultant refused to have the interview recorded.

The interviews with the consultants were longer than those with the chiefs-of-staff, averaging 92 minutes. I had two main goals with the consultant interviews. The first was to get an idea about how "connected" they were with the affairs of the party. By connected I mean the level of interaction not only with the party's formal apparatus, but also the extent to which they held key positions in the informal network of office holders and staffers as they went about their business in the election. The second goal was to use the interviews with the consultants as a "reality check" against what the staffers had already told me. Not that I believed that the chiefs-of-staff were particularly prone to lying, but I was aware of the sensitive nature of some of the questions that I was asking. In addition, staffers operate in a different environment than that of the political consultant, relying on a different set of experiences and expectations to evaluate the political world.

THE COUNTY PARTY CHAIRMEN

Sample

The sample of party chairs was drawn from five counties in Southern California—Los Angeles, Orange, Ventura, Riverside, and San Bernardino counties. All of the parties' chairs were contacted by mail and interview times and locations were finalized by phone. All of the chairs agreed to be interviewed for the study.

Conducting the Interviews

All of the interviews were taped. The interviews took place in a diverse set of locations. Because many of these county parties lacked a permanent headquarters (this was particularly true for the Democrats), the interviews were conducted in restaurants, businesses, and in their homes. The average length of the interviews was 83 minutes.

These interviews were particularly important because I was concerned that political staffers and consultants might have been elevating or exaggerating their role in the political process. I did not see this as a deliberate attempt to mislead me, but it is probably natural for these players to feel that the political universe revolves around them and that the process lives or dies based on their participation. The party chairs were, therefore, used not only to provide an important perspective on the formal apparatus of the party, but also as a way of confirming the information provided me by the staffers and consultants. By and large, the process, as described by the staffers and consultants, was similar to that revealed by the party chairs. Even in those instances when staffers and consultants were critical of the role played by the statutory party, the party chairs agreed with those assessments.

Appendix B

P resented below are the instruments used for the Chief-of-Staff study. Though each instrument enabled me to quantify many of the responses, many questions were designed with an open-ended format to elicit the maximum amount of information. Credit for many of the questions is owed to John Petrocik who generously allowed me to use questions that he had developed for another survey.

CHIEF-OF-STAFF QUESTIONNAIRE

Background

1. How did you get your job as field director?
2. How long ago did you become involved in politics?
3. Did someone or some group play an important part in causing you to become involved in politics or did you become involved on your own?

Constituency Service

1. To help me better understand who does what in these offices, could we go down a list of the staff and talk about what each person does?
2. What percent of the staffs' time is allotted to casework?
3a. What types of citizen problems occupy the majority of the staffs' time? What specific problems?
3b. Do you ever take on constituency cases that deal with another governmental jurisdiction?

3c. What type of problems?
4. How are these problems divided among the staff? How do you decide which staffers handle certain problems?
5. When you think of the specific concerns of your district, do you divide it into different areas? Into different groups? Why do you do it this way?
6a. Do you ever work with the *staffs* of other office holders on constituency service activities?
6b. (For each mention) What projects do you work on?
7a. Do you ever work with the *staffs* of other office holders on election-related activities?
7b. (For each mention) What projects do you work on?
8. Do you have regularized meetings with other staffers in the area?

Informants

1. If a friend who wanted to run for public office in this area came to you for advice, which person(s) would you suggest that he talk with before making a final decision?
   Is there any individual or group who might be really helpful to his or her success?
2. I am interested in how you learn about political developments in the area. Could you tell me something about the people who help to keep you informed about important issues?
   Who is the *most important person* you rely on to keep track of things?
   Do you ever work with this person? What do you work on?
   Who is the *second most important person* you rely on to keep track of things?
   Do you ever work with this person? What do you work on?

Campaigns

1. Am I safe in assuming that you and other staff members help on the campaign on your own time? Is that the entire staff?
2a. What workers did you have in your district in the last election helping out on the campaign? Did you use workers from another field office?
2b. (If mentioned) You mentioned that you used workers from other offices. How was the work of these people directed?

3. What kinds of campaign activities did the workers in your office perform in the last election? What specific activities?

4a. Have you or your office staff ever helped out in other candidates' campaigns? What office was being sought? Were there any others?

4b. What kind of help was it? Was this during the primary or general election?

4c. Who requested that your office supply support or did you decide to support on your own?

4d. What made you decide to aid this candidate?

5a. Do you meet or talk with *party officials* during the campaign? Which ones(s)?

Recruitment

1a. Have you ever encouraged someone to run for office for the *first* time? What office was it? Were there any others that you encouraged?

1b. Did you or your staff *personally* give any of these candidates any help in his/her campaign? What kind of help was it? Was this during the primary or general election?

1c. Who requested that your office supply support *or* did you decide to support on your own?

1d. Have you ever discouraged a first time candidate from seeking office? Who?

2a. Have you ever encouraged an established office holder to seek higher office? What office was it? Were there any others that you encouraged?

2b. Did you or your staff *personally* give any of these candidates any help in his/her campaign? What kind of help was it? Was this during the primary or general election?

2c. Who requested that your office supply support *or* did you decide to support on own?

2d. Have you ever discouraged an elected official from seeking higher office? Who?

3. Does any member of the staff hold a formal party position? Which one?

4a. Have you or any member of your staff run for political office? Which one(s)?

4b. Did your office provide any kind of support? What kind?

5. Do you have any aspirations for public office? Which office?

6. Has a consultant ever become a member of your staff *or* has a member of your staff taken a job as a consultant?

CONSULTANT QUESTIONNAIRE
Background

1. How long ago did you become involved in politics?
2. How did you get started working on campaigns?
3. Did someone or some group play an important part in causing you to become involved in politics or did you become involved on your own?
4. Have you ever held a position in a governmental office? Which position(s)?
5. Have you ever worked on the staff of an elected official? Which one(s)?
6. Have you ever held a leadership position in the party?
7. Would you like to hold public office some day?
8. Do you have any interest in holding a position of leadership in the party?

Campaigns

1. What kinds of services go directly to the party?
2. Do you ever provide services to candidates?
3. Do you work exclusively for one of the parties or have you worked for candidates from both parties? (*If they work for only one party*) Why do you work exclusively for one party?
4. How many campaigns have you been involved in over the last three years? What kinds of offices were being sought?
5. Other than specific work for candidates, what other types of campaign work did you perform in the last election cycle?
6. Do you earn your entire living from working on campaigns? (*If not*) What else do you do?
7a. What impact do you think that Proposition 140 will have on campaigns? How about the quality of candidates for office?
7b. Do you think that it will increase or decrease the amount of money spent on campaigns? Why?
8. There has been a great deal of attention paid to the effect of the new techniques used in campaigns, however many campaigns continue to include attempts to make personalized contacts with voters through door-to-door canvassing and the like. Is there still a role for old-fashioned campaign techniques?

9. Is there a difference between the way Democrats and Republicans use their institutional resources of the party in campaigns?
10. What is the party's role in contemporary campaigns?
11. What new techniques can we expect to see in the future?

Informants

1. If a friend who wanted to run for public office in this area came to you for advice which person(s) would you suggest that he talk with before making a final decision?
   Is there any individual or group who might be really helpful to his or her success?
2. I am interested in how you learn about political developments in the area. Could you tell me something about the people who help to keep you informed about important issues?
   Who is the *most important person* you rely on to keep track of things?
   Do you ever work with this person? What do you work on?
   Who is the *second most important person* you rely on to keep track of things?
   Do you ever work with this person? What do you work on?

Office Holders, Staffs, and Party Officials

1a. Which *office holders* do you talk or work with on a fairly regular basis?
1b. (For each mention) What projects do you work on?
2a. How about their *staffs*, do you ever work with the *staffs* of these office holders?
2b. (For each mention) What projects do you work on?
3a. Which *party officials* do you meet or work with on a fairly regular basis?
3b. (For each mention) What projects do you work on?

Recruitment

1a. Have you ever encouraged someone to run for office for the *first* time? What office was it? Were there any others that you encouraged to run for office the first time?
1b. Did you *personally* give any of these candidates any help on his/her campaign? What kind of help was it? Was this during the primary or general election? Were you paid?

1c. Who requested that you supply support *or* did you decide to support on your own? What made you decide to aid this candidate?
1d. Have you ever discouraged a first time candidate from seeking office? Who?
2a. Have you ever encouraged an *established* office holder to run for another office? What office was it? Were there any others that you encouraged?
2b. Did you personally give any of these candidates any help in his/her campaign? What kind of help was it? Was this during the primary or general election? Were you paid?
2c. Who requested that you supply support *or* did you decide to support on your own? What made you decide to aid this candidate?
2d. Have you ever discouraged an elected official from seeking higher office? Who?

PARTY CHAIRMEN QUESTIONNAIRE

Background

1. How did you get your position as party chairman?
2. How long ago did you become involved in politics?
3. Did someone or some group play an important part in causing you to become involved in politics or did you become involved on your own?
4. Have you ever held a position in a governmental office? Which position(s)?
5. Have you ever worked on the staff of an elected official? Which one(s)?
6. Would you like to hold public office some day?

Campaigns

1a. In the last election cycle, which campaigns received a majority of the party's resources?
1b. What type of services did the party provide?
2. Other than specific work for candidates, what other types of campaign work did the party perform in the last election cycle?
3a. What impact do you think that Proposition 140 will have on campaigns? How about the quality of candidates for office?
3b. Do you think that it will increase or decrease the amount of money spent on campaigns? Why?
4. There has been a great deal of attention paid to the effect of the new techniques used in campaigns, however many campaigns continue

to include attempts to make personalized contacts with voters through door-to-door canvassing and the like. Is there still a role for old-fashioned campaign techniques?
5. Is there a difference between the way Democrats and Republicans use the institutional resources of the party in campaigns?
6. What is the party's role in contemporary campaigns?

Informants

1. If a friend who wanted to run for public office in this area came to you for advice, which person(s) would you suggest that he talk with before making a final decision?
   Is there any individual or group who might be really helpful to his or her success?
2. Could you tell me something about the people who help to keep you informed about important issues?
   Who is the *most important person* you rely on to keep track of things?
   Do you ever work with this person? What do you work on?
   Who is the *second most important person* you rely on to keep track of things?
   Do you ever work with this person? What do you work on?

Office Holders, Staffs, and Consultants

1a. Which *office holders* do you talk or work with on a fairly regular basis?
1b. (*For each mention*) What projects do you work on?
2a. How about their *staffs*, do you often meet with the *staffs* of these office holders?
2b. (*For each mention*) What projects do you work on?
3. By in large, staffers who are involved in campaigns report little contact with the party. Why is this?
4. What impact do you think staffers who get involved in campaigns have on the process?
5a. Which *consultants* do you talk or work with on a fairly regular basis?
5b. (*For each mention*) What projects do you work on?
6. What impact do you think political consultants have on the campaign process?
7. Consultants tend to deemphasize your role in campaigns. Is this a fair assessment?

Recruitment

1a. Have you ever encouraged someone to run for office for the *first* time? What office was it? Were there any others who you encouraged to run for office the first time?

1b. Did the *party* give any of these candidates any help on his/her campaign? What kind of help was it? Was this during the primary or general election?

1c. Who requested that you supply support *or* did the party decide to support on your own? What made you decide to aid this candidate?

1d. Have you ever discouraged a first time candidate from seeking office? Who?

2a. Have you ever encouraged an *established* office holder to run for another office? What office was it? Were there any others that you encouraged?

2b. Did the *party* give any of these candidates any help in his/her campaign? What kind of help was it? Was this during the primary or general election? Were you paid?

2c. Who requested that you supply support *or* did the party decide to support on your own? What made you decide to aid this candidate?

2d. Have you ever discouraged an elected official from seeking higher office? Who?

3. What are some party-building strategies that you would like to initiate in the future?

4. Working on the staff of an elected official appears to the predominate vehicle for anyone interested in public office. Why is this so?

Appendix C

STAFF INTERVIEWS, 1992

Congressional Districts

Robert Lagomarsino (19th-R)
William Thomas (20th-R)
Elton Gallegly (21st-R)
Carlos Moorehead (22nd-R)
Anthony Beilenson (23rd-D)
Henry Waxman (24th-D)
Edward Roybal (25th-D)
Howard Berman (26th-D)
Mel Levine (27th-D)
Julian Dixon (28th-D)
Maxine Waters (29th-D)
Matthew Martinez (30th-D)
Mervyn Dymally (31st-D)
Glen Anderson (32nd-D)
David Dreier (33rd-R)
Esteban Torres (34th-D)
Jerry Lewis (35th-R)
George Brown (36th-D)
Alfred McCandless (37th-R)
Robert Dornan (38th-R)
William Dannemeyer (39th-R)
Dana Rohrabacher (42nd-R)

State Assembly Districts

Philip D. Wyman (34-R)
Cathie Wright (36-R)
Paula Boland (38th-R)
Richard Katz (39th-D)
Tom Bane (40th-D)
Pat Nolan (41st-R)
Dick Mountjoy (42nd-R)
Terry Friedman (43rd-D)
Tom Hayden (44th-D)
Burt Margolin (45th-D)
Barbara Friedman (46th-D)
Teresa Hughes (47th-D)
M. Archie-Hudson (48th-D)
Gwen Moore (49th-D)
Curtis Tucker (50th-D)
Gerald Felando (51st-R)
Paul Horcher (52th-R)
Dick Floyd (53th-D)
Willard Murray (54th-D)
Richard Polanco (55th-D)
Lucille Roybal-Allard (56th-D)
Dave Elder (57th-D)
Tom Mays (58th-R)
Xavier Becerra (59th-D)
Sally Tanner (60th-D)
William Lancaster (62nd-R)
Bob Epple (63rd-D)
Jim Brulte (65th-R)

Notes

CHAPTER 1. AMERICAN POLITICAL PARTIES

1. This term, to the best of my knowledge, was first used by Robert H. Salisbury and Kenneth Shepsle in (1981a) "U.S. Congressmen as Enterprises." *Legislative Studies Quarterly.* 6:559–76.

2. This study is based on several sources. The first is a project conducted at UCLA with my colleagues Dwaine Marvick, John R. Petrocik, and Fernando Guerra in the winter of 1990 (hereafter referred to as the *Field Office Study*). The project conducted interviews with over 300 field staffers working for incumbents from Congress, the California State Senate and State Assembly, the Los Angeles County Board Supervisors, and the Los Angeles City Council. In all, over 100 offices took part in the study in the Southern California area. The second source is additional interviews that I conducted in the winter of 1992 (hereafter referred to as the *Chief-of-Staff Interviews*). These interviews were designed to supplement the information gathered in the first study and provide greater detail on Los Angeles party politics. These interviews were conducted with the chiefs-of-staff in the field offices for members of Congress and the State Assembly in Los Angeles County. Together, I interviewed fifty chiefs-of-staff, twenty-two from congressional offices and twenty-eight from the California State Assembly.

CHAPTER 2. THE MEANING OF PARTY

1. Joseph Schlesinger (1984) provides a thorough justification for excluding voters from the conceptualization of the party. See also E. E. Schattschneider's similar exclusion of voters. He writes, "Whatever else the parties may be, they are not associations of the voters who support the party candidates" (1942, 53).

CHAPTER 3. THE PARTY WEB

1. The mean number of district-based staff for members of Congress in 1959 was .9, and by 1999, this figure had risen to 9.6.

2. Few legislators were defeated. In the state's history before 1965, only 161 out of 3,055 (4.3%) members of the Assembly had been defeated in a reelection attempt. In the Senate, the figure is 86 out of 892 (9.6%).

3. Staff figures provided by *The California State Government Directory* (Sacramento: California Journal, 1999).

4. The state law forbidding pre-primary party endorsements was repealed in 1989.

CHAPTER 4. POLITICAL STAFFING

1. Alan Ehrenhalt's book, *The United States of Ambition* (1992), presents a thorough, case-by-case analysis of this change. For a similar view of Congress, see Burdett Loomis, *The New American Politician* (1988).

2. Since Schlesinger's 1966 book, *Ambition and Politics*, there have been numerous efforts to expand and apply the concept of political ambition in American politics. Its propositions have been applied to the genesis of political aspirations (Fowler and McClure 1989; Kazee 1980) and politicians' responses to formal opportunities for advancement (Black 1970; Fishel 1971). Ambition theory has been applied to specific institutions such as Congress, concentrating on members' desires for the office itself and as a launching point for higher office (Kernell 1977; Peabody, Ornstein, and Rhode 1976; Jacobson and Kernell 1983; Salisbury and Shepsle 1981b; Canon 1990; Mezey 1970; Bullock 1972). Others have focused on how political ambition has affected the behavior of politicians (Prewitt 1970; Rhode 1979; Hibbing 1986). These same concepts have also been applied to state and local politics (Tobin 1975; Robeck 1982; Squire 1988; Schwartz 1990; Tobin and Keyes 1975; Keyes, Tobin, and Danziger 1979; Hain 1976; Northrop and Dutton 1978).

3. For an exception, see John D. Macartney 1975. *Political Staffing: A View from the District.* Ph.D. Dissertation. University of California, Los Angeles.

4. In this instance, former aides or staffers were counted if they fell into several different categories: 1) having worked for an elected official, 2) having worked as a staffers for any of the legislative committees, or 3) having worked as an aide for the Legislative Caucus.

5. The same categories were used to identify members of Congress as former aides.

6. These figures were compiled from the *Congressional Quarterly Almanac*, 1974–1999.

7. Information based on interview number 101 (state legislative aide).
8. Information based on interview number 022 (congressional aide).

CHAPTER 5. THE ENTERPRISE-IN-OFFICE

1. This aspect of the enterprise-in-office will be discussed in the next chapter.
2. *Los Angeles Times*, (Monday, October 29, 1990):A15.
3. *Los Angeles Times*, (Monday, October 29, 1990):A16.
4. For an alternative perspective, one that focuses on resource acquisition, see Ruth S. Jones and Thomas J. Borris (1985) and Jeffrey M. Stonecash (1988).
5. Chiefs-of-staff working for freshmen officeholders were asked if they worked on the incumbent's campaign for that office.
6. Information based on interview number 101 (state legislative aide).
7. United States Congress, Committee on Rules and Administration, 92nd Congress, 1971. The Hatch Act (1939) forbids government officials from engaging in political activity. Many staffers described their job as really consisting of two jobs: their government job in the district office and their job as a campaign worker.
8. Campaigning was clearly going on during my visits to the field office. During the interview, the chiefs-of-staff took phone calls from fundraisers, pollsters, and other campaign specialists. Most were quite open about these activities.
9. The division of staff time ranged from those who were employed one-third in the field office and two-thirds in the campaign to two-thirds devoted to the field office and one-third to the campaign. Equal division of time was fairly common. Information based on interview numbers 108 (state legislative aide), 115 (state legislative aide), 120 (state legislative aide), 012 (congressional aide), 001 (congressional aide), and 101 (state legislative aide).
10. Information based on interview number 022 (congressional aide).
11. Information based on interview number 120 (state legislative aide).
12. Information based on interview number 101 (state legislative aide).
13. Information based on interview number 108 (state legislative aide).
14. This figure is derived from a number of different sources. Federal staff figures can be found in the *Congressional Staff Directory* (Washington, D.C.: Annual Edition). State figures can be found in *The California State Government Directory* (Sacramento: California Journal, 1999). And figures for city and county governments were provided by the *Los Angeles County Roster* (Los Angeles: The Los Angeles County Registrar of Voters, 1999). Excluded from the totals are volunteers working in the various field offices.
15. Information based on interview number 021 (congressional aide).

16. Information based on interview number 125 (state legislative aide).
17. Information based on interview number 115 (state legislative aide).
18. Information based on interview numbers 128 (state legislative aide), 106 (state legislative aide), 108 (state legislative aide), 115 (state legislative aide), 101 (state legislative aide), 124 (state legislative aide), 018 (congressional aide), 001 (congressional aide), and 012 (congressional aide).
19. Information based on interview number 015 (congressional aide).
20. Information based on interview number 108 (state legislative aide).
21. Information based on interview numbers 117 (state legislative aide), 114 (state legislative aide), 124 (state legislative aide), 110 (state legislative aide), 101 (state legislative aide), 020 (congressional aide), 018 (congressional aide), and 006 (congressional aide).
22. Information based on interview number 006 (congressional aide).
23. Information based on interview number 112 (state legislative aide).

CHAPTER 6. THE PARTY NETWORK

1. An office was counted as coordinating election plans with another if the respondent reported cooperating with another office on any aspect of the campaign. This could entail sharing direct mail costs, sponsoring a joint fund-raiser, or mobilizing mutual constituent groups.
2. Information based on interview numbers 020 (congressional aide), 001 (congressional aide), 110 (state legislative aide), 113 (state legislative aide), 008 (congressional aide), and 126 (state legislative aide).
3. Information based on interview numbers 116 (state legislative aide), 120 (state legislative aide), 021 (congressional aide), and 001 (congressional aide).
4. The same method was used here as in Table 5.1.
5. Information based on interview numbers 104 (state legislative aide) and 012 (congressional aide).
6. The interviews were conducted prior to the 1992 California primaries, thus staffers were asked to characterize their involvement in the 1988 general election.
7. Information based on interview number 109 (state legislative aide).
8. Information based on interview numbers 026 (congressional aide), 023 (congressional aide), 118 (state legislative aide), and 111 (state legislative aide).
9. Information based on interview number 127 (state legislative aide).
10. Information based on interview numbers 024 (congressional aide) and 026 (congressional aide).

11. Information based on interview numbers 103 (state legislative aide), 106 (state legislative aide), and 110 (state legislative aide).

12. Information based on interview numbers 101 (state legislative aide), 104 (state legislative aide), and 107 (state legislative aide).

13. For the purposes of this test, lending from one white office holder to another was not counted as an ethnic "match."

14. Information based on interview number 107 (state legislative aide).

15. Information based on interview number 114 (state legislative aide).

CHAPTER 7. MINI-MACHINES

1. Information based on interview numbers 017 (congressional aide), 011 (congressional aide), and 124 (state legislative aide).

2. Information based on interview numbers 001 (congressional aide), 011 (congressional aide), and 009 (congressional aide).

3. These figures are not based on an accurate tabulation of case types. Congressional and State Assembly staffers were asked to give an estimate of how the individual cases were distributed. The percentages are averages for each office type, federal and state.

4. Information based on interviews numbers 124 (state legislative aide) and 121 (state legislative aide).

5. Many incumbents hold monthly Open Houses in the district. This gives constituents a chance to meet the incumbent personally. Often, constituents attend to request the legislator's aid or thank the legislator for the successful resolution of their case.

6. Information based on interview numbers 109 (state legislative aide), 118 (state legislative aide), 110 (state legislative aide), 102 (state legislative aide), 013 (congressional aide), and 012 (congressional aide).

7. Information based on interview number 114 (state legislative aide).

8. Information based on interview numbers 118 (state legislative aide) and 121 (state legislative aide).

9. Information based on interview number 105 (state legislative aide).

10. Information based on interview number 123 (state legislative aide).

11. Information based on interview number 011 (congressional aide).

12. Information based on interview numbers 128 (state legislative aide), 008 (congressional aide), 016 (congressional aide), and 007 (congressional aide).

13. Information based on interview number 011 (congressional aide).

14. Information based on interview number 124 (state legislative aide).

15. Information based on interview number 124 (state legislative aide).

16. Information based on interview number 008 (congressional aide).

17. Information based on interview number 015 (congressional aide).

18. Information based on interview numbers 123 (state legislative aide), 126 (state legislative aide), 124 (state legislative aide), and 022 (congressional aide).

Bibliography

Abrahamsson, Bengt. 1977. *Bureaucracy or Participation: The Logic of Organization.* London: Sage Publications.

Adkisson, John. 1979. "Staff Assistant Today, Assembly Member Tomorrow." In T. Anthony Quinn and Ed Salzman, eds. *California Public Administration.* Sacramento: California Journal Press.

Agranoff, Robert. 1972. *The New Style in Election Campaigns.* Boston: Holbrook Press.

Ainsworth, Bill. 1993. "Battle of the Branches." *California Journal.* 24:21–23.

Aldrich, John H. 1995. *Why Parties? The Origins and Transformation of Party Politics in America.* Chicago: University of Chicago Press.

Alston, Chuck. 1991. "Members with Cash on Hand Reach Out to Help Others." *Congressional Quarterly Weekly Report.* (September 29): 2763–2766.

American Political Science Association's Committee on Political Parties. 1950. *Toward a More Responsible Two-Party System.* New York: Holt, Rinehart, and Wilson.

Anders, Evan. 1982. *Boss Rule in South Texas: The Progressive Era.* Austin: University of Texas Press.

Arterton, G. Christopher. 1982. "Political Money and Political Strength." In Joel L. Fleishman, ed. *The Future of American Political Parties.* Englewood Cliffs, NJ: Prentice Hall.

Backstrom, Charles H. 1986. "The Legislature as a Place to Work: How Minnesota Legislators View their Jobs." Hubert H. Humphery Institute of Public Affairs. University of Minnesota.

Barrilleaux, Charles. 1986. "A Dynamic Model of Partisan Competition in the American States." *American Journal of Political Science.* 30:882–40.

Bean, Walter. 1967. *Boss Ruef's San Francisco.* Berkeley: University of California Press.

Beard, Charles A. 1915. *Economic Origins of Jeffersonian Democracy*. New York: Macmillan.

Berke, Richard L. 1989. "Incumbents Turn to Personal PACs." *New York Times*. (June 16):A11.

Binkley, Wilfred. 1958. *American Political Parties: Their Natural History* 3d ed. New York: Alfred A. Knopf.

Black, Gordon. 1970. "A Theory of Professionalization in Politics." *American Political Science Review*. 64:864–78.

Block, A. G. and Claudia Buck. 1999. *California Political Almanac 1999–2000*. Sacramento, CA: State Net Services & Publications.

Bonafede, Dom. 1982. "Ideological and Tactical Differences Spice Wirth v. Bucchner House Race." *National Journal*. (July 17):1599.

Broder, David. 1972. *The Parties Over: The Failure of Politics in America*. New York: Harper & Row.

Brown, Roscoe, and Ray Smith. 1922. *Political and Governmental History of the State of New York*. Syracuse: Syracuse University Press.

Bryce, James. 1959. *The American Commonwealth*. ed. Louis Hacker. New York: Putman. 1888 reprint.

Bullock, Charles S., III. 1972. "House Careerist: Changing Patterns of Longevity and Attrition." *American Political Science Review*. 66:1294–1305.

Burnham, Walter Dean. 1982. *The Current Crisis in American Politics*. New York: Oxford University Press.

Burnham, Walter Dean. 1970. *Critical Elections and the Mainsprings of American Politics*. New York: Norton.

Burnham, Walter Dean. 1969. "The End of American Party Politics." *Transaction*. 7:12–22.

Cain, Bruce, John Ferejohn, and Morris Fiorina. 1987. *The Personal Vote*. Cambridge: Harvard University Press.

Caldeira, Gregory, and Samuel C. Patterson. 1982. "Bringing Home the Votes: Electoral Outcomes in State Legislative Races." *Political Behavior*. 4:33–67.

Callow, Alexander B. 1966. *The Tweed Ring*. New York: Oxford University Press.

Canon, David T. 1990. *Actors, Athletes, and Astronauts: Political Amateurs in the Unites States Congress*. Chicago: University of Chicago Press.

Chambers, William M. 1963. *Political Parties in a New Nation*. New York: Oxford University Press.

Clark, Peter B. and James Q. Wilson. 1961. "Incentive Systems: A Theory of Organizations." *Administrative Science Quarterly*. 6:219–66.

Coleman, John J. 1994. "The Resurgence of Party Organization? A Dissent from the New Orthodoxy." In *The State of the Parties: The Changing*

Role of Contemporary American Parties. ed. Daniel M. Shea and John C. Green. Lanham, MD: Rowman & Littlefield.

Coleman, John J. 1996. "The Resurgence or Just Busy? Party Organization in Contemporary America." In *The State of the Parties: The Changing Role of Contemporary American Parties.* ed. John C. Green and Daniel M. Shea. 2d. ed. Lanham, MD: Rowman & Littlefield.

Commager, H. S. 1950. "The American Political Party." *American Scholar.* 19:309–16.

Connors, Richard J. 1971. *Cycle of Power.* Metuchen, NJ: The Scarecrow Press.

Cotter, Cornelius P., James L. Gibson, John F. Bibby, and Robert J. Huckshorn. 1984. *Party Organizations in American Politics.* New York: Praeger.

Cotter, Cornelius P., and John F. Bibby. 1980. "Institutional Development of Parties and the Thesis of Party Decline." *Political Science Quarterly.* 95:1–27.

Cotter, Cornelius P., and Bernard Hennessy. 1964. *Politics Without Power: The National Party Committees.* New York: Atherton Press.

Crotty, William, ed. 1986. *Political Parties in Local Areas.* Knoxville: University of Tennessee Press.

Crotty, William. 1985. *The Party Game.* San Francisco: W. H. Freeman & Co.

Crotty, William. 1984. *American Parties in Decline.* Second Edition. Boston: Little, Brown.

Crotty, William. 1971. "Party Effort and Its Impact on the Vote." *American Political Science Review.* 65:439–50.

Crotty, William. 1970. "Political Parties Research." In Michael Haas and Henry Kariel, eds. *Approaches to the Study of Political Science.* San Francisco: Chandler.

Crotty, William, and Gary C. Jacobson. 1980. *American Parties in Decline.* Boston: Little, Brown.

Dennis, Jack. 1980. "Changing Public Support for the American Party System." In William Crotty, ed. *Paths to Political Reform.* Lexington, MA: Lexington Books/D.C. Health.

Dillin, John. 1989. "Leaders' Personal PACs Draw Fire." *Christian Science Monitor.* (June 23):7.

Downs, Anthony. 1957. *An Economic Theory of Democracy.* New York: Harper and Brothers.

Dutton, William H. 1975. "The Political Ambitions of Local Legislators: A Comparative Perspective." *Polity.* 8:504–22.

Duverger, Maurice. 1954. *Political Parties.* New York: John Wiley & Sons, Inc.

Edsall, Thomas B. 1989. "Branching Out with Burgeoning Influence." *Washington Post.* (January 17):11.

Edsall, Thomas B. 1986. "More than Enough is Not Enough." *Washington Post National Weekly Edition.* (February 9):16.

Ehrenhalt, Alan. 1992. *The United States of Ambition.* New York: Times Books.

Eldersveld, Samuel J. 1982. *Political Parties in American Society.* New York: Basic Books.

Eldersveld, Samuel J. 1964. *Political Parties.* Chicago: Rand McNally.

Epstein, Leon D. 1986. *Political Parties in the American Mold.* Minneapolis: The University of Wisconsin Press.

Epstein, Leon D. 1983. "The Scholarly Commitment to Parties." In Ada Finifter, ed. *Political Science: The State of the Discipline.* Washington, DC: American Political Science Association.

Epstein, Leon D. 1967. *Political Parties in Western Democracies.* New Brunswick, NJ: Transaction.

Erie, Stephen P. 1988. *Rainbow's End.* Berkeley: University of California Press.

Federal Election Commission. 1998. *Campaign Finance Reports.*

Fenno, Richard F., Jr. 1978. *Home Style: House Members in their Districts.* Boston: Little, Brown.

Fiorina, Morris P. 1977. *Congress: Keystone of the Washington Establishment.* New Haven: Yale University Press.

Fish, C. R. 1904. *The Civil Service and Patronage.* Cambridge: Harvard University Press.

Fishel, Jeff. 1979. *Parties and Elections in an Anti-Party Age.* Bloomington, Indiana: Indiana University Press.

Fishel, Jeff. 1971. "Ambition and the Political Vocation." *Journal of Politics.* 33:24–56.

Fowler, Linda L., and Robert D. McClure. 1989. *Political Ambition: Who Decides to Run for Congress.* New Haven: Yale University Press.

Fox, Harrison W., Jr., and Susan Webb Hammond. 1977. *Congressional Staffs.* New York: The Free Press.

Frantzich, Stephen E. 1989. *Political Parties in the Technological Age.* New York: Longman.

Frendreis, John P. 1996. Voters, Government Officials, and Party Organizations: Connections and Distinctions." In *The State of the Parties: The Changing Role of Contemporary American Parties.* ed. John C. Green and Daniel M. Shea. 2d. ed. Lanham, MD: Rowman & Littlefield.

Frendreis, John P. and Alan R. Gitelson. 1998. "Local Parties in the 1990s: Spokes in a Candidate-Centered Wheel." In *The State of the Parties:*

The Changing Role of Contemporary American Parties. ed. John C. Green and Daniel M. Shea. 3d. ed. Lanham, MD: Rowman & Littlefield.

Frendreis, John P., James L. Gibson, and Laura L. Vertz. 1990. "The Electoral Relevance of Local Party Organization." *American Political Science Review.* 84:224–35.

Fritz, Sara, and Dwight Morris. 1990. "Campaign Cash Takes a Detour." *Los Angeles Times.* (October 28):A1.

Gibson, James L., Cornelius P. Cotter, John F. Bibby, and Robert J. Huckshorn. 1985. "Wither the Local Parties?: A Cross-Sectional and Longitudinal Analysis of the Strength of Party Organizations." *American Journal of Political Science.* 29:139–60.

Gibson, James L., Cornelius P. Cotter, John F. Bibby, and Robert J. Huckshorn. 1983. "Assessing Party Organizational Strength." *American Journal of Political Science.* 27:193–222.

Gimpel, James. 1996. *National Elections and the Autonomy of American State Party Systems.* Pittsburgh: University of Pittsburgh Press.

Goldberg, Eddie N., and Michael W. Traugott. 1984. *Campaigning for Congress.* Washington, DC: Congressional Quarterly Press.

Gosnell, Harold. 1937. *Machine Politics: Chicago Model.* Chicago: The University of Chicago Press.

Gosnell, Harold. 1924. *Boss Platt and His New York Machine.* Chicago: The University of Chicago Press.

Green, Stephen, ed. 1992. *California Political Almanac.* Sacramento: California Journal.

Guterbock, Thomas S. 1980. *Machine Politics in Transition.* Chicago: University of Chicago Press.

Hain, Paul L. 1976. "Constituency Characteristics, Political Ambition, and Advancement." *American Politics Quarterly.* 27:264–74.

Herring, Pendleton. 1965. *The Politics of Democracy.* New York: Norton.

Herrnson, Paul. 1986. "Do Parties Make a Difference? The Role of Party Organization in Congressional Elections." *Journal of Politics.* 48:589–615.

Hershey, Marjorie Randon. 1984. *Running for Office: The Political Education of Campaigners.* Chatham, NJ: Chatham House.

Hershkowitz, Leo. 1977. *Tweed's New York.* New York: Anchor Press.

Hibbing, John R. 1986. "Ambition and the House: Behavioral Consequences of Higher Office Goals among U.S. Representatives." *American Journal of Political Science.* 30:651–65.

Hirsch, Mark. 1948. *William C. Whitney, Modern Warwick.* New York: Norton.

Huckshorn, Robert J. 1976. *Party Leadership in the States.* Amherst: University of Massachusetts Press.

Jacobson, Gary C. 1987. *The Politics of Congressional Elections*. Second Edition. Boston: Little, Brown.

Jacobson, Gary C., and Samuel Kernell. 1983. *Strategy and Choice in Congressional Elections*. New Haven: Yale University Press.

Janda, Kenneth. 1980. *Political Parties: A Cross-National Survey*. New York: The Free Press.

Jeffe, Sherry Bebitch. 1987. "For Legislative Staff, Policy Takes a Backseat to Politics." *California Journal*. 18:42–45.

Jewell, Malcolm E. 1986. "A Survey of Campaign Find-raising by Legislative Parties." *Comparative State Politics Newsletter*.

Jewell, Malcolm E. 1982. *Representation in State Legislatures*. Lexington: University of Kentucky Press.

Jewell, Malcolm E., and David M. Olson. 1988. *Political Parties and Elections in American States*. Chicago: The Dorsey Press.

Jewell, Malcolm E., and David M. Olson. 1982. *American State Political Parties and Elections*. Homewood, IL: The Dorsey Press.

Jewell, Malcolm E, and Samuel C. Patterson. 1986. *The Legislative Process in the United States*. New York: Random House.

Jones, Ruth S., and Thomas J. Borris. 1985. "Strategic Contributing in Legislative Campaigns: The Case of Minnesota." *Legislative Studies Quarterly*. 10:89–105.

Kayden, Xandra, and Eddie Mahe, Jr. 1987. *The Party Goes On: The Persistence of the Two-Party System in the United States*. New York: Basic Books.

Kazee, Thomas. 1980. "The Decision to Run for the U.S. Congress: Challengers' Attitudes in the 1970s." *Legislative Studies Quarterly*. 5: 79–100.

Kent, Frank R. 1923. *The Great Game of Politics*. Garden City, NY: Doubleday, Page and Company.

Kernell, Samuel. 1977. "Toward Understanding Congressional Careers: Ambition, Competition, and Rotation." *American Journal of Political Science*. 21:669–93.

Kessel, John H. 1984a. *Presidential Campaign Politics*. Homewood, IL: The Dorsey Press.

Kessel, John H. 1984b. *Presidential Parties*. Homewood, IL: The Dorsey Press.

Key, V. O., Jr. 1964. *Politics, Parties, and Pressure Groups*. Fifth Edition. New York: Crowell-Collier.

Key, V. O., Jr. 1956. *American State Politics: An Introduction*. New York: Alfred A. Knopf.

Key, V. O., Jr. 1949. *Southern Politics*. New York: Alfred A. Knopf.

Keyes, Edward W., Richard J.Tobin, and Robert Danziger. 1979. "Institutional Effects in Elite Recruitment: The Case of State Nominating Systems." *American Politics Quarterly.* 7:283–302.

Kirchheimer, Otto. 1966. "The Transformation of Western European Party Systems." In Joseph LaPalombara and Myron Weiner, eds. *Political Parties and Political Development.* Princeton: Princeton University Press.

Kirkpatrick, Evron M. 1971. "Toward a More Responsible Two-Party System: Political Science, Policy Science or Pseudo Science?" *American Political Science Review.* 65:964–90.

Kirkpatrick, Jeane. 1977. *Dismantling the Parties.* Washington DC: American Enterprise Institute.

Kofmehl, Kenneth T. 1977. *Professional Staffs of Congress.* West Lafayette, IN: The Purdue University Press.

Kurtz, Howard. 1987. "Congress is a Convenient Place to Stockpile Campaign Aides." *Washington Post National Weekly Edition.* (July, 13):13.

Ladd, Everett Carll, and Charles D. Hadley. 1975. *Transformations of the American Party System.* New York: Norton.

Ladd, Everett Carll 1978. *Where Have All the Voters Gone?* New York: Norton.

Lewis, Alfred H. 1901. *Richard Croker.* New York: Life Publishing Co.

Lewis, Catherine. 1991. "The Proposition 140 Aftermath." *California Journal.* 22:249–54.

Lindblom, Charles E. 1965. *The Intelligence of Democracy.* New York: Free Press.

Loftus, Tom. 1985. "The New 'Political Parties' in State Legislatures." *State Government.* 58:108.

Longley, Charles H. 1980. "National Party Renewal." In Gerald M. Pomper, ed. *Party Renewal in America.* New York: Praeger.

Loomis, Burdett. 1988. *The New American Politician.* New York: Basic Books.

Loomis, Burdett. 1979. "Setting Course: A Congressional Office as a Small (?) Business." *Publius.* 9:51–57.

Luntz, Frank. 1988. *Candidates, Consultants, and Campaigns.* Oxford: Basil Blackwell.

Lynch, Denis T. 1927. *"Boss" Tweed.* New York: Boni and Liveright.

Macartney, John D. 1987. "Congressional Staff: The View from the District." In David C. Kozak, ed. *Congress and Public Policy.* Chicago: The Dorsey Press.

Macartney, John D. 1975. *Political Staffing: A View from the District.* Ph.D. Dissertation. University of California, Los Angeles.

MacIver, Robert M. 1926. *The Modern State.* London: Oxford University Press.

Macridis, Roy C. 1967. "Introduction." In Roy C. Macridis, ed. *Political Parties*. New York: Harper & Row.

Malbin, Michael J. 1980. "The Republican Revival." *Fortune.* (August 25):85.

Malbin, Michael J. 1979. *Unelected Representatives*. New York: Basic Books.

Mandelbaum, Seymour J. 1965. *Boss Tweed's New York*. New York: John Wiley & Sons.

Marvick, Dwaine. 1990. "Legislative Field Staff Workers in the Los Angeles Area: Their Careers, Concerns, and Collaborative Efforts." Paper presented at the 1990 Annual Meeting of the Western Political Science Association.

Marvick, Dwaine, John R. Petrocik, Fernando Guerra, and J. P. Monroe. 1990. *Field Office Study*. University of California, Los Angeles.

Marvick, Dwaine. 1974. "Communication in Political Parties." In Ithiel de Sola Pool and Wilbur Schramm, eds. *Handbook of Communication*. Chicago: Rand McNally. Chapter 23.

Matthews, Donald R. 1960. *U.S. Senators and Their World*. New York: John Wiley & Sons.

Matthews, Donald R. 1954. *The Social Backgrounds of Political Decision-Makers*. New York: Random House.

Mayhew, David R. 1986. *Placing Parties in American Politics*. Princeton: Princeton University Press.

Mayhew, David R. 1974. *Congress: The Electoral Connection*. New Haven: Yale University Press.

McCloskey, Herbert. 1964. "Consensus and Ideology in American Politics." *American Political Science Review.* 58:361–82.

Merton, Robert. 1957. *Social Theory and Social Structure*. Glencoe, IL: Free Press.

Mezey, Michael. 1970. "Ambition Theory and the Office of Congressman." *Journal of Politics.* 32:563–579.

Michels, Robert. 1949. *Political Parties*. trans. Eden and Cedar Paul. Glencoe, IL: The Free Press.

Miller, Alan C., and Dwight Morris. 1992. "Manhattan Outpaces L.A. as Provider of Political Money." *Los Angeles Times.* (January 26):A26.

Miller, Alan C. 1990. "California Alliance's Cumulative Generosity is Unmatched in Congress." *Los Angeles Times.* (Monday, October 29, 1990):A16.

Miller, Alan C., and Dwight Morris. 1992. "Playing Fast with Loose Spending Rules." *Los Angeles Times.* (November 1):A3.

Miller, Warren E., and M. Kent Jennings. 1986. *Parties in Transition*. New York: Russell Sage.

Miller, Zane L. 1968. *Boss Cox's Cincinnati*. New York: Oxford University Press.

Mushkat, Jerome. 1971. *Tammany*. Syracuse: Syracuse University Press.

Myers, Gusttavus. 1917. *The History of Tammany Hall*. New York: Boni and Liveright.

National Conference of State Legislatures. 1998. *Legislative Staff Services: 50 State Profiles 1998*. Lexington.

National Conference of State Legislatures. 1986. *State Legislators' Occupations: A Decade of Change*. Lexington.

Neumann, Sigmund. 1956. "Toward a Comparative Study of Political Parties." In Sigmund Neumann, ed. *Modern Political Parties*. Chicago: Chicago University Press.

Nie, Norman H., Sidney Verba, and John R. Petrocik. 1979. *The Changing American Voter*. Cambridge: Harvard University Press.

Northrop, Alan, and William H. Dutton. 1978. "Municipal Reforms and Group Differences." *American Journal of Political Science*. 22:691–711.

Novak, Michael. 1971. *The Rise of the Unmeltable Ethnics*. New York: Macmillan.

Olson, Mancur. 1965. *The Logic of Collective Action*. Cambridge: Harvard University Press.

Oreskes, Michael. 1987. "Tandem Jobs: Legislative and Campaigns." *New York Times*. (September 19): A1.

Ornstein, Norman J., Thomas E. Mann, and Michael J. Malbin. 2000. *Vital Statistics on Congress*. Washington, DC: American Enterprise Institute.

Ostrogorski, M. 1902. *Democracy and the American Party System*. New York: Macmillan.

Parenti, Michael. 1967. "Ethnic Politics and the Persistence of Ethnic Identification." *American Political Science Review*. 61:716–26.

Parsons, Talcott. 1956. "Suggestions for a Sociological Approach to the Theory of Organizations—I, II." *Administrative Science Quarterly*. 1:63–85, 224–39.

Patterson, Samuel C., and Gregory Caldeira. 1984. "The Etiology of Party Competition." *American Political Science Review*. 78:691–707.

Peabody, Robert L., Norman J. Ornstein, and Davis W. Rhode. 1976. "The United States Senate as Presidential Incubator: Many are Called but Few are Chosen." *Political Science Quarterly*. 91:236–58.

Peel, Roy V. 1935. *The Political Clubs of New York*. New York: G.P. Putman.

Petrocik, John R. 1981. *Party Coalitions*. Chicago: Chicago University Press.

Pitkin, Hannah. 1967. *The Concept of Representation*. Berkeley: University of California Press.

Polsby, Nelson. 1983. *Consequences of Party Reform*. New York: Oxford University Press.

Polsby, Nelson. 1968. "The Institutionalization of the U.S. House of Representatives." *American Political Science Review*. 62:144–68.

Polsby, Nelson, and Aaron Wildavsky. 1984. *Presidential Elections: Strategies of American Electoral Politics*. Sixth Edition. New York: Scribners.

Pomper, Gerald M. 1977. "The Decline of Party in American Elections." *Political Science Quarterly*. 92:21–42.

Pomper, Gerald M. 1971. "Toward a More Responsible Party System? What, Again?" *Journal of Politics*. 33:915–40.

Prewitt, Kenneth. 1970a. "Political Ambitions, Volunteerism, and Electoral Accountability." *American Political Science Review*. 64:4–17.

Prewitt, Kenneth. 1970b. *Recruitment of Political Leaders*. Indianapolis: Bobbs Merrill.

Price, David E. 1984. *Bringing Back the Parties*. Washington, DC: Congressional Quarterly Press.

Rakove, Milton. 1975. *Don't Make No Waves—Don't Back No Losers*. Bloomington: Indiana University Press.

Ranney, Austin. 1975. *Curing the Mischiefs of Faction*. Berkeley: California University Press.

Ranney, Austin, and Willmoore Kendall. 1956. *Democracy and the American Party System*. New York: Harcourt, Brace & World.

Rapoport, Ronald B., Alan I. Abramowitz, and John McGlennon. 1986. *The Life of the Parties*. Lexington: University Press of Kentucky.

Reichley, A. James. 1985. "The Rise of National Parties." *The New Direction in American Politics*. In John E. Chubb and Paul E. Peterson, eds. Washington, DC: Brookings.

Reynolds, George M. 1936. *Machine Politics in New Orleans*. New York: Columbia University Press.

Rhode, David W. 1979. "Risk-Bearing and Progressive Ambition: The Case of Members of the United States House of Representatives." *American Journal of Political Science*. 23:1–26.

Riordon, William L. 1963. *Plunkitt of Tammany Hall*. New York: E.P. Dutton. 1905 reprint.

Richardson, James. 1989. "Legislative Clout." *California Journal*. 20:347–52.

Richardson, James. 1988. "Rewards of Working for the Legislature." *California Journal*. 19:110–12.

Riker, William. 1962. *The Theory of Political Coalitions*. New Haven: Yale University Press.

Robeck, Bruce W. 1982. "State Legislator Candidacies for the U.S. House: Prospects for Success." *Legislative Studies Quarterly*. 7:506–14.

Roberts, Steven V. 1981. "Another New Twist to the Games the PAC Men Play." *New York Times*. (August 12):A24.

Rosenthal, Alan. 1989. "The Legislative Institution: Transformed and at Risk." In Carl E. Van Horn, ed. *The State of the States*. Washington, DC: Congressional Quarterly Press.

Sabato, Larry. 1983. "Parties, PACs, and Independent Groups" In Thomas Mann and Norman Ornstein, eds. *The Election of 1982.* Washington, DC: American Enterprise Institute.

Sabato, Larry. 1981. *The Rise of Political Consultants.* New York: Basic Books.

Sait, Edward M. 1927. *American Politics Parties and Elections.* New York: Century Co.

Salisbury, Robert H., and Kenneth Shepsle. 1981a. "U.S. Congressmen as Enterprises." *Legislative Studies Quarterly.* 6:559–76.

Salisbury, Robert H., and Kenneth Shepsle. 1981b. "Congressional Staff Turnover and the Ties-That-Bind." *American Political Science Review.* 75:381–96.

Salmore, Stephen A., and Barbara G. Salmore. 1989. "The Transformation of State Electoral Politics." In Carl E. Van Horn, ed. *The State of the States.* Washington, DC: Congressional Quarterly Press.

Salmore, Stephen A., and Barbara G. Salmore. 1985. *Candidates, Parties, and Campaigns.* Washington, D.C.: Congressional Quarterly Press.

Salter, John T. 1935. *Boss Rule: Portraits in City Politics.* New York: McGraw-Hall.

Schattschneider, E. E. 1975. *The Semisovereign People.* Hinsdale, IL: Dryden Press.

Schattschneider, E. E. 1942. *Party Government.* New York: Rinehart.

Schlesinger, Joseph A. 1991. *Political Parties and the Winning of Office.* Ann Arbor: University of Michigan Press.

Schlesinger, Joseph. 1985. "The New American Party System." *American Political Science Review.* 79:1152–169.

Schlesinger, Joseph. 1984. "On the Theory of Party Organization." *Journal of Politics.* 46:369–400.

Schlesinger, Joseph. 1966. *Ambition and Politics.* Chicago: Rand McNally.

Schlesinger, Joseph. 1965. "Political Party Organization." In J. G. March, ed. *Handbook of Organizations.* Chicago: Rand McNally.

Schumpeter, Joseph A. 1947. *Capitalism, Socialism, and Democracy.* New York: Harper and Brothers.

Schwartz, Mildred A. 1990. *The Party Network: The Robust Organization of Illinois Republicans.* Madison: University of Wisconsin Press.

Seligman, Lester. 1971. *Recruiting Political Elites.* New York: General Learning Press.

Shea, Daniel M. 1995. *Transforming Democracy: Legislative Campaign Committees and Political Parties.* Albany: State University of New York Press.

Sorauf, Frank. 1984. *Party Politics in America.* New York: Little, Brown.

Sorauf, Frank. 1967. "Political Parties and Political Analysis." In William Nisbet Chambers and Walter Dean Burnham, eds. *The American Party*

Systems: Stages of Political Development. New York: Oxford University Press.

Sorauf, Frank, and Paul Allen Beck. 1988. *Party Politics in America*. Sixth Edition. Glenview, IL: Scott Foresman.

Squire, Peverill. 1988. "Career Opportunities and Membership Stability in Legislatures." *Legislative Studies Quarterly*. 13:64–82.

Starkey, Danielle. 1993. "Saving the Legislative Analyst." *California Journal*. 24:13–16.

Stave, Bruce M. 1970. *The New Deal and the Last Hurrah*. Pittsburgh: Pittsburgh University Press.

Stoddard, Lothrop. 1931. *Master of Manhattan*. New York: Longmans, Green and Co.

Stonecash, Jeffery M. 1988. "Working at the Margins: Campaign Finance and Strategy in New York Assembly Elections." *Legislative Studies Quarterly*. 13:476–493.

Sullivan, Terry. 1984. *Procedural Structure*. New York: Praeger.

Sundquist, James T. 1981. *The Decline and Resurgence of Congress*. Washington, DC: Brookings.

Thomas, Lately. 1962. *A Debonair Scoundrel*. New York: Holt, Rinehart and Winston.

Tobin, Richard J. 1975. "The Influence of Nominating Systems on the Political Experience of State Legislators." *Western Political Quarterly*. 12: 94–107.

Tobin, Richard J., and Edward W. Keyes. 1975. "Institutional Differences in the Recruitment Process: A Four State Study." *American Journal of Political Science*. 19:666–82.

Tocqueville, Alexis de. 1945. *Democracy in America*. vol. 1. New York: Alfred A. Knopf.

Volger, David. 1974. *The Politics of Congress*. Boston: Allyn and Bacon.

Watson, Tom. 1985. "Machines: Something Old, Something New." *Congressional Quarterly Weekly Report*. (August 17):1619.

Wattenberg, Martin. 1998. *The Decline of American Political Parties: 1952–1998*. Cambridge: Harvard University Press.

Wattenberg, Martin. 1984. *The Decline of American Political Parties: 1952–1980*. Cambridge: Harvard University Press.

Weber, Max. 1958. "Politics as a Vocation." In *From Max Weber: Essays in Sociology*. H. H. Gerth and C. Wright Mills, eds. and trans. New York: Oxford University Press.

Weberg, Brian. 1988. "Changes in Legislative Staff." *The Journal of State Government*. 61:190–98.

Werner, Morris R. 1928. *Tammany Hall*. New York: Doubleday, Doran and Co., Inc.

Wilson, James Q. 1973. *Political Organizations*. New York: Basic Books.

Wilson, James Q. 1966. *The Amateur Democrat*. Chicago: University of Chicago Press.

Wolfinger, Raymond E. 1972. "Why Political Machines Have Not Withered Away and Other Revisionist Thoughts." *Journal of Politics*. 34:364–98.

Wolfinger, Raymond E. 1965. "The Development and Persistence of Ethnic Voting." *American Political Science Review*. 59:895–908.

Wright, William E. 1971. "Comparative Party Models: Rational Efficient and Party Democracy." In William E. Wright, ed. *A Comparative Study of Party Organization*. Columbus: Merrill.

Index